Celebration of Steam:
The Chilterns
Laurence Waters

IAN ALLAN *Publishing*

First published 1995

ISBN 0 7110 2377 8

Published by Ian Allan Publishing

an imprint of Ian Allan Ltd, Terminal House, Station Approach, Shepperton, Surrey TW17 8AS.
Printed by Ian Allan Printing Ltd, Coombelands House, Coombelands Lane, Addlestone, Weybridge, Surrey KT15 1HY.

Acknowledgements

I would like to thank the following individuals and associations for supplying photographs and other material for this book: D. Trevor Rowe, John Edwards, George Hine, Peter Stears, Mike Soden, Hugh Ballantyne, Brian Morrison, Hugh Harman, Ken Fairey and Courtney Haydon.

Also, many pictures have been obtained from The Great Western Trust Collection and the Ian Allan Library.

Special thanks to Dr Jim Boudreau for information regarding workings and to Dane Garrod for reading and offering suggestions on the manuscript.

Contents

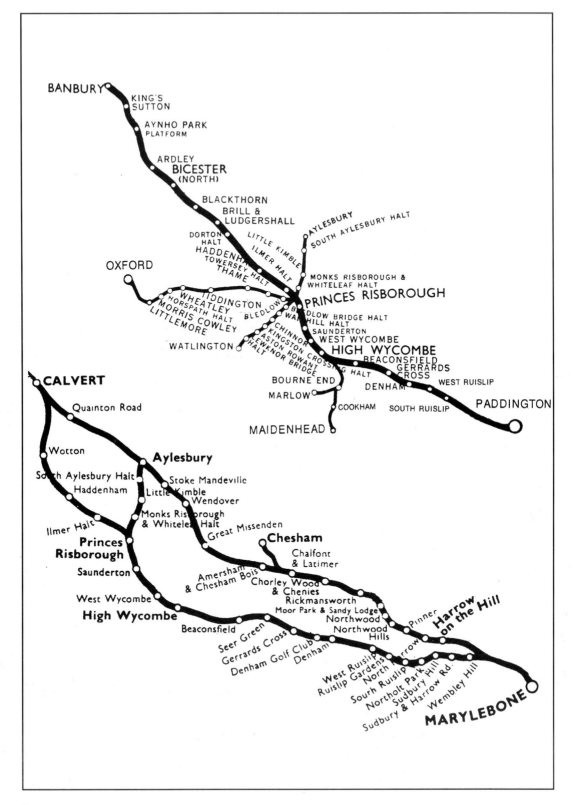

Introduction

The Chilterns provide one of the most scenic areas in the Home Counties. The beechwoods around High Wycombe spawned a furniture-making industry which even today forms an important part of the manufacturing output of the area. The hills themselves run from east to west across the southern end of the shire counties of Buckingham and Oxford. The chalk hills that make up the Chiltern escarpment were once dissected by four main lines: the Great Western, the Great Central, the Midland and the London & North Western. All four still survive, but today only the ex-London & North Western line from Euston, which passes through the hills via a deep cutting at Tring, and the Midland line from St Pancras, which skirts the hills to the east, still match the main line description. Although both pass through The Chilterns, neither has really had the same association with the area as the ex-Great Central and Great Western lines. The remains of the old Great Central and Metropolitan joint line from Marylebone to the north still threads its way through the hills to Quainton Road and Calvert, but passenger services now terminate at Aylesbury. It was this section that during the early part of the century was promoted by the Metropolitan Company as 'Metroland', resulting in the railway gradually spreading the commuter belt out across the Buckinghamshire countryside as far as Aylesbury.

The ex-Great Western and Great Central joint line to Princes Risborough and the ex-GW 'cut-off' section to Banbury have in recent years become a through route to Birmingham once again, but much of the line has been downgraded and beyond Princes Risborough singled; for the purpose of this book I have covered these latter two lines and their associated branches which were, and still are, known as the 'Chiltern lines'.

I was very pleased when Ian Allan asked me to produce this book as I have many personal memories of the area. Living in Oxford I can well remember many trips to Aylesbury during the mid-1950s to see the 'A3s', 'V2s' and 'B1s' as well as the 'L1' tanks. Because of the cost of the train fare the trips were made using a City of Oxford Motor Services 'Express Service' AEC single-deck bus, painted aptly in chocolate and cream. These buses actually departed from the station forecourt and took just under an hour to complete the 23-mile journey. The first 'A3' I ever saw, No 60102 *Sir Frederick Banbury*, on the up 'Master Cutler' service, was seen on a spotting trip to Aylesbury.

Shed trips with the local railway club included several visits to Neasden, Woodford Halse and Leicester Central. My own visits to the joint line were limited; I preferred instead to travel up the line to Banbury where one 'saw more'. However, it must be said that the sight and sound of a 'King' or an 'A3' blasting its way up Saunderton Bank or speeding down through Princes Risborough was something to savour. On a sadder note I can well remember standing on Bicester North station on Friday 11 June 1965 watching the last scheduled steam passenger service over the line arrive behind No 7029 *Clun Castle*.

I have selected the photographs for this book from the post-Nationalisation period. They have certainly brought back many memories to me of these two interesting routes and I hope also to you, the reader, of those glorious days of steam in The Chilterns.

Above left: **Map showing ex-Great Western 'Chiltern' lines and branches covered in the book.**

Below left: **Map showing area covered by ex-GC suburban services from Marylebone.**

Right: **The end of the line for the 2.50pm from Princes Risborough at Watlington, Hauled by WR 0-6-0 PT No4680 in June 1957, During the last month of passenger services on the branch.**
J. M. Beaspark.

1. The Growth of the Chiltern Lines

The ex-Great Western 'cut-off' route from Paddington to Birmingham via High Wycombe, although opened on 1 July 1910, was unusual as it was not planned from the word go by the Great Western as a main route but gradually evolved over a period of 56 years by a mixture of new construction and improvements to existing lines. High Wycombe saw its first trains on 1 August 1854 with the opening by the Wycombe Railway Co of a 9¾-mile broad-gauge branch from Maidenhead. This single-line branch ran via Bourne End and connected at Maidenhead with the Great Western main line to the west. The Wycombe Railway was soon expanding and on 1 August 1862 the branch was extended along the picturesque River Wye valley through to the market towns of Princes Risborough and Thame. Princes Risborough became a junction station on 1 October 1863 with the opening of its 7½-mile branch to Aylesbury. On 24 October 1864 the Thame branch was extended through to Kennington Junction just to the south of Oxford. Thus, the early seeds of the eventual 'cut-off' route had been sown. The Wycombe Railway route from Oxford to Maidenhead and London was actually eight miles shorter than the established route via Didcot Junction and Reading. The Princes Risborough-Aylesbury branch was converted to standard gauge between 13 and 23 October 1868. At Aylesbury the branch connected with the standard gauge Aylesbury & Buckingham Railway. The Aylesbury

& Buckingham had been opened on 23 September 1868; initially built as a single-track railway (it was doubled in 1892), it ran between Aylesbury, Quainton Road and Verney Junction where it connected with the Buckinghamshire Railway's route from Bletchley to Oxford. The line was operated under a working agreement by the Great Western until it was absorbed by the Metropolitan Railway on 1 July 1891.

The rest of the Wycombe Railway was not converted from broad to standard gauge until 1870, the work taking place between 23 August and 1 September. During the 1890s the Great Western was looking at ways of shortening some of its routes. At this time there was great competition between the Great Western and the London & North Western over traffic to Birmingham. Unfortunately, the Great Western route to Birmingham and Wolverhampton via Oxford had a considerable mileage disadvantage over the LNWR line, and, in 1897, to try and even things up the Company promoted a new line which would run from the GW main line at Acton and connect with the existing Maidenhead-Kennington Junction branch at High Wycombe. It was envisaged at this time that the existing single line between Wycombe, Princes Risborough and Kennington Junction would be doubled and upgraded. The new route would effectively shorten the distance to Birmingham by about eight miles.

The next stage in the development of the 'Chiltern lines' was the decision in 1891 by the Manchester, Sheffield & Lincolnshire Railway to promote a bill for a 92-mile-long 'London Extension' from Annesley Junction to link up with the Metropolitan line at Quainton Road. From here the MS&LR would run the 40 miles to Neasden over the newly-completed Metropolitan lines. This latter arrangement was made possible because at the time of the proposal Sir Edward Watkin was the chairman of both the MS&LR and the Metropolitan. It seems that it may have been Watkin's intention that once the MS&LR had established its southern link, it would take over the Metropolitan.

The Metropolitan Railway, which had been incorporated in 1853, had extended its 'main line' northwards, reaching Harrow-on-the-Hill on

Above left: **Oxford (81F)-allocated '6100' class 2-6-2T No 6111 arrives at Princes Risborough in April 1962 with a service from Oxford. For many years services to and from Oxford were worked by the 2-6-2Ts. No 6111 was actually the longest serving postwar Oxford engine, being allocated to the shed from August 1949 until it was withdrawn on 31 December 1965.** *D. Loveday*

Left: **Another view of No 6111 on the 1.58pm service to Oxford on the penultimate day of passenger services, 5 January 1963. Waiting in the siding is '1600' class 0-6-0PT No 1622 on the Chinnor Cement Works coal train.** *S. Boorne*

Left: **The first station on the Oxford branch after leaving Risborough was at Bledlow, pictured here on 25 August 1962 as '6100' class No 6124 (81F) arrives with the 7.50pm service from Oxford.**
Great Western Trust

Centre left: **With Bledlow station in the background BR Standard Class 9F No 92220 *Evening Star* runs past with the LCGB 'Six Counties Railtour' on 3 April 1960. The special originated at Paddington and ran via Maidenhead, High Wycombe, Oxford, Bletchley and Luton before terminating at Broad Street.**
Courtney Haydon

Below left: **On the same day ex-GW '7200' class 2-8-2T No 7238 from Oxford (81F) approaches the station with an eastbound engineers' train. The three Oxford-based members of the class were regular performers over the 'Risborough Branch'.**
Courtney Haydon

Above right: **An unidentified '6100' class 2-6-2T arrives at Towersey Halt with a service from Oxford. The halt was opened on 5 June 1933.**
J. D. Edwards

Below right: **The main intermediate station on the branch was at Thame. The station, which contained a fine Brunel-designed overall roof, was opened by the Wycombe Railway on 1 August 1862. Just over 100 years later on 25 August 1962 '6100' class No 6149 (81F) stands at Thame with the 1.20pm service from Oxford to Princes Risborough.**
R. C. Riley

Left: **Another superb shot of Thame taken on 4 February 1962 shows fellow class member No 6156 (81F) on the Sundays-only 10am service from Oxford to Princes Risborough.** *Bryan Jennings*

Below left: **The other main intermediate station and crossing point was at Wheatley. The station is pictured here on a very snowy 5 January 1963, the penultimate day of passenger services over the branch. '6100' class 0-6-2T No 6106 departs with the 2.42pm service to Princes Risborough as fellow class member No 6111 arrives with the late running 1.58pm service to Oxford.** *S. Boorne*

Above right: **On a sunny summer's day in 1962 '6100' class 2-6-2t No 6156 (81F) stands at Wheatley with the 1.58pm service from Princes Risborough. The station porter, Percy White, looks rather worried as he makes his way over to the down platform.** *A. Simpkins*

Centre right: **'5100' class 2-6-2T No 4147 (81F) approaches Morris Cowley on Sunday 11 September 1960 with the 5.50pm service from Oxford to Princes Risborough. In the background is part of the Morris car factory at Cowley, since demolished.** *M. Mensing*

Below right: **At the Oxford end the branch joined the main line at Kennington Junction (branch on the right). Here in the early 1950s 'Modified Hall' No 6970 *Whaddon Hall* (81F) speeds past the junction on the 10.25am Sundays-only stopping service to Didcot.** *R. H. G. Simpson*

2 August 1880, Rickmansworth on 1 September 1887 and Aylesbury, the most important town in the area, on 1 September 1892. At first the Metropolitan ran to a temporary station at Brook Street but, on 1 January 1894, the line was extended into the existing joint station at Aylesbury, where it connected with the Aylesbury & Buckingham Railway and the Great Western.

The Manchester, Sheffield & Lincolnshire Railway had been formed in 1864 by the amalgamation of several smaller companies. Until the construction of its main line to London, the company had operated an east-west route over the Pennines to the east coast.

Powers for the MS&LR to construct its London Extension were obtained by an Act of 28 March 1893, and under a further Act of 1 August 1897 the company changed its name to the Great Central Railway. Soon after the new line was started, agreement was reached with the Great Western to construct an eight-mile branch connecting the new line at Culworth, just south of Woodford Halse, to the existing GW Birmingham route, just north of Banbury. The construction of this branch which opened on 1 August 1900 was undertaken by the Great Central, but was actually financed by the Great Western.

In May 1894 John Bell succeeded Watkin as Chairman of the Metropolitan and immediately complained about the joint working arrangement over the Metropolitan section. This unsatisfactory situation took a new turn when the Great Central and the Great Western held talks to look into the feasibility of taking over the construction of the Acton-Wycombe line as a joint venture. The Great Western supported the idea as the cost of

the proposed Acton-Wycombe section would be shared. The Great Central also saw the new line as an alternative to using the far from satisfactory Metropolitan route via Wendover, Amersham and Rickmansworth into London. The new GW/GC joint committee was formed on 1 August 1899 with power to take over the construction of the Acton-Wycombe line between Northolt and Wycombe. North of Wycombe, the old Wycombe Railway route to Princes Risborough would be doubled and a new 15-mile-long section constructed between here and Grendon Underwood where it would connect with the Great Central's London Extension. At the southern end a junction would be built at Northolt and new lines would be constructed to Neasden to give access to the Great Central terminus at Marylebone. Construction was started on the seven-mile GW section between Old Oak Common West Junction and Greenford in January 1901. The first section of the new line was opened to Park Royal on 15 June 1903 and to Greenford on 1 October 1904. Meanwhile, the joint section was progressing well and the whole line, including the 6¼-mile GC section from Neasden to Northolt, was opened for goods traffic through to Grendon Underwood on 20 November 1905, and with the construction of the main stations complete the new line was opened for passenger traffic on 2 April 1906. Although constructed by the joint committee, the section from Ashendon to Grendon Underwood became from 20 November 1905 the property of the Great Central.

The Great Central's own London Extension was opened to passengers on 15 March 1899;

Above left: **The junction was controlled by Kennington Junction signalbox, which is seen here on 3 May 1953 as ex-LMS Class 5 No 44771 from Bletchley (1E) on a diverted Bletchley to Marylebone parcels train starts its 1 in 80 climb up to Littlemore.** *R. H. G. Simpson*

Above: **Another view at Kennington Junction shows ex-Great Western '4300' class 2-6-0 No 5370 from Tyseley (84E) passing the junction signalbox on 10 May 1951 with an up goods from Hinksey yard. The box here unusually faced the branch rather than the main line.** *R. H. G. Simpson*

Right: **Branch services terminated at Oxford. On 2 July 1960 '7200' class 2-8-2T No 7218 (81F) enters Hinksey yard with the daily freight from Honeybourne. In the background is the gas works (now demolished) which at one time had its own private railway.** *K. L. Cook*

interestingly, history records that the first service to depart from Marylebone — the 5.15am to Manchester — left with just four passengers. Ironically, by the time the joint line was under construction the differences between the Great Central and the Metropolitan Railway had been resolved, resulting in the formation on 2 April 1906 of the Metropolitan & Great Central Joint Committee to administer the running of the Metropolitan lines south of Quainton. Great Central suburban services had commenced running between Marylebone and Aylesbury on 1 March 1906.

It was probably soon after the the construction of the joint line had started that the Great Western abandoned the idea of upgrading the old Wycombe Railway branch from Princes Risborough to Oxford and decided instead to construct a more direct route northwards across the slightly easier terrain of the Vale of Aylesbury. Powers to construct the new line were obtained in 1905. The new line which was known as the 'Bicester Cut-Off' had the additional advantage of a further 11-mile reduction in the distance to Birmingham over the original proposal via Thame and Kennington Junction and left the joint line via a junction at Ashendon. From here it ran via Bicester to connect with the Oxford–Birmingham line via a flying junction at Aynho. The new 'cut-off' line was opened for passengers on 1 July 1910 and gave an overall reduction of some 19 miles over the old Didcot and Oxford route.

Below left: **On 18 June 1954 'County' class 4-6-0 No 1018** *County of Leicester* **(84A) prepares to depart with the 8.42am service from Wolverhampton to Portsmouth Harbour. Standing at the down platform on station pilot duty is 'Hall' No 4938** *Liddington Hall* **(81F). Diesel Railcar No W7W is running through to the north bay where it will form a service to Worcester.** *Author's Collection*

Bottom left: **'6100' class 2-6-2T No 6154 (81B) stands at Oxford in the summer of 1962 with the 12.52pm service to Princes Risborough comprising just two coaches. On the left the south station pilot is 'Hall' class No 6927 Lilford Hall (81F). Once the Risborough train departs, the three-car DMU will form the next train to Reading.** *S. Boorne*

Above right: **With the many cross-country services, Oxford was a mecca for the railway enthusiast right up until the end of steam. Here on 4 September 1965 ex-SR 'Battle of Britain' class 4-6-2 No 34060** *25 Squadron* **departs with the 8.30am service from Newcastle to Bournemouth. Waiting in the up through road is Standard Class 9F 2-10-0 No 92231 on a Banbury-Hinksey freight.** *I. M. Slater*

Centre right: **The locomotive shed at Oxford, opened in the 1850s, was extended in 1864 but was never rebuilt by the Great Western. The wonderful wooden structure can be seen here on 18 July 1963. Locomotives in view are, left to right, '2884' class 2-8-0 No 3862 (Cardiff East Dock), '5700' class 0-6-0PT No 9653 (81F) and 'Hall' class 4-6-0 No 5957** *Hutton Hall* **(81F). Oxford was the last Western Region steam shed to close on 31 December 1965.** *Great Western Trust*

Below: **A fine view of 'Britannia' class 4-6-2 No 70054** *Dornoch Firth* **as it stands in the yard at Oxford on 9 June 1963. At this time 'Britannias' were the regular motive power on the Morris Cowley-Bathgate car trains.** *D. Tuck*

Above: **Intermediate stations on the 'cut-off' route between Banbury, Princes Risborough and High Wycombe were served by a number of auto-trains. On 23 July 1958 Banbury (84C)-allocated 0-6-0PT No 5420 enters Ilmer Halt with the 6pm service from Banbury to Princes Risborough. The auto service from Banbury was inaugurated with the opening of the 'cut-off' route in July 1910, the services remaining a feature of the line until they were withdrawn on 16 June 1962. Ilmer Halt was opened by the GW on 1 April 1929 and closed on 7 January 1963.** *M. Mitchell*

Below: **Bicester North is the main intermediate station on the section between Princes Risborough and Aynho. On 26 May 1962 the Princes Risborough-Banbury 'Auto' service calls at Bicester hauled by '5100' class 2-6-2T No 5101 (84C). The station has in recent years been completely refurbished.** *D. Trevor Rowe*

Above: **'Hall' class No 5994** *Roydon Hall* **from Worcester (85A) picks up the slip coach from the 5.10pm fast service from Paddington to Wolverhampton at Bicester North on 25 August 1960. The coach will be attached to the 4.34pm semi-fast service to Wolverhampton seen standing at the platform. The Bicester slip was the last slip coach working in the country, coming to an end on 9 September 1960.**
M. Mensing

Right: **The 'cut-off' route joined the Oxford-Birmingham main line at Aynho Junction. Here on 23 April 1960 No 6003** *King George IV* **(81A) crosses the flyover bridge at Aynho with the 8.30am service from Paddington to Wolverhampton. The Oxford line can be seen behind the trees.** *R. C. Riley*

Below right: **The main station at Aynho, Aynho for Deddington, was situated on the old Oxford-Birmingham line. Opened in 1852 the down buildings are still standing and have recently been sold as a private dwelling. On 31 July 1956 'Hall' class No 5981** *Frensham Hall* **from Shrewsbury (84G) speeds through with the 8.35am service from Newcastle to Bournemouth West.**
H. Gordon Tidey

Left: '6100' class 2-6-2T No 6159 (81F), on the 3.50pm service from Oxford to Banbury, passes Aynho Junction on 29 August 1962. The junction signalbox can be seen on the right as can the up and down 'cut-off' lines. The junction box has in recent years been closed, and the junction is now controlled from Marylebone. *M. Mensing*

Centre left: A down freight hauled by '2800' class 2-8-0 No 2836 leaves the Oxford line at Aynho Junction on 29 August 1962. Passing on an up service via the 'cut-off' route is the 11.40am Birkenhead-Paddington train hauled by diesel-hydraulic No D1035 *Western Yeoman*. *M. Mensing*

Below: Looking northwards, an up fitted freight for the Oxford line approaches Aynho Junction on 29 August 1962 behind 'Modified Hall' No 6987*Shervington Hall* (84A). *M. Mensing*

Above right: From Aynho Junction services ran along the original Oxford & Birmingham railway route to Banbury. Just north of the junction were Aynho water troughs, where on 19 May 1962 'Castle' class No 5067 *St Fagans Castle* (81D) speeds over the troughs with the 10.50am service from Wolverhampton to Margate. *A. A. Vickers*

Below right : Looking south on the same day, 'King' No 6029 *King Edward VIII* (81A) speeds over the troughs with the down 'Cambrian Coast Express', the 11.10am service from Paddington to Aberystwyth and Pwllheli. *A. A. Vickers*

Above: **The low winter sun picks out an unidentified BR Standard Class 9F 2-10-0 as it heads a limestone train from Ardley Quarry to Greaves Sidings over the water troughs at Aynho in February 1966. The use of redundant ironstone wagons on these services has regularly seen them wrongly described as ironstone trains.** *A. Muckley*

Left: **'Grange' class 4-6-0 No 6811 *Cranbourne Grange* from Stourbridge (2C) accelerates away from Kings Sutton with the 3.25pm all-stations stopping service from Banbury to Oxford on 15 April 1963.** *Hugh Ballantyne*

Below right: **Slightly over the top on motive power, a down limestone service from Ardley Quarry to Greaves Sidings comprising three wagons and a guard's van approaches Astrop sidings south of Banbury hauled by '9F' No 92234 on 22 May 1965.** *Mike Soden*

Above: **A Shrewsbury-allocated 'Hall' class 4-6-0 No 6916** *Misterton Hall* **approaches Kings Sutton with the 10.45am through service from Poole to Sheffield on 29 August 1964. The line on the right is the remains of the through route** **from Banbury to Kingham and Cheltenham which closed to passengers between Chipping Norton and Banbury on 4 June 1951.** *W. L. Underhay*

Above: **At the northern extremity of the Chiltern Lines is Banbury. On 24 May 1962 '5100' class 2-6-2T No 4171 from Leamington shed coasts past the locomotive yard at Banbury with another limestone train from Ardley Quarry to Greaves Sidings.** *Great WesternTrust*

Left: **The locomotive shed at Banbury was opened in September 1908 and contained four roads. In September 1963 regional boundary changes saw the depot pass to London Midland Region control. On 27 June 1965 the occupants are ex-LMS '8F' No 48414 from Leicester, Class 5 No 45045 from Shrewsbury and, inside, '9F' No 92002 from Tyseley. The shed was closed to steam on 3 October 1966.** *Mike Soden*

Below left: **Another view shows a pair of Banbury-allocated '9F' 2-10-0s Nos 92203 and 92215 standing at the back of the shed on 20 June 1965. The large building on the right is the lifting shop, constructed during 1944.** *Mike Soden*

Above right: **'Grange' Class 4-6-0 No 6848 Toddington Grange from Worcester (85A) departs from Banbury on 27 March 1965 with the 10.8am service from York to Bournemouth West. No 6848 was one of the last 'Granges' to survive, being withdrawn from Worcester on 31 December 1965.** *Brian Stephenson*

Right: **A view of Banbury in 1959 with 'Hall' class No 6929 Whorlton Hall (84A) waiting in the down bay. The rebuilt station had been completed the previous year. Notice the engine is in lined green but still carries the old BR emblem.** *J. D. Edwards*

Left: **York (50A)-allocated ex-LNER 'V2' No 60847** *St Peters School York AD 627* **departs from Banbury in March 1964 with the 10.50am service from Bournemouth West to York. This service ran via Banbury Junction and Woodford Halse.**
Mike Soden

Left: **The same location and service, but on 4 July 1964 motive power is in the hands of Crewe (5A)-allocated BR Standard Class 9F No 92120. The photographer has remarked in his notes that the '9F' was unusual motive power on this service.**
Mike Soden

Below: **The final shot of Banbury was taken on 1 January 1966, and shows Croes Newydd (6C)-allocated ex-LMS Class 5 No 45198 making a spectacular start with the 10.8am service from York to Bournemouth.**
G. P. Cooper

2. Ex-Great Central Services and Motive Power

During the period covered by this book a considerable change took place on both the services and the motive power used on Chiltern area lines. Over the ex-Great Central section during the 1950s many of the through services from Marylebone to Sheffield and Manchester were still in the hands of ex-LNER locomotives. The ex-Great Central express passenger types had been replaced by the newer 'B1' 4-6-0s, 'V2' 2-6-2s and 'B17' 'Footballer' 4-6-0s. These latter locomotives were not altogether successful on GC services and were all allocated away during 1952/53. The heaviest services at this time were hauled by ex-LNER 'A3' Pacifics allocated to both Neasden and Leicester Central. Although a few 'A3s' had worked on the line before World War 2 it was not until February 1949 that they appeared in any numbers. In 1954 there were 12 working on the line. These were not the best examples of the class, but the consistently good performances that were obtained were a credit to the Leicester and Neasden loco-crews.

Prior to World War 2 there were 12 services daily between Marylebone and Manchester. By the mid-1950s this had been reduced to just six down and five up services each day comprising three to Sheffield and Manchester, one to Sheffield, one to Bradford and one through service to Liverpool via Sheffield and Manchester. The up trains comprised one from Liverpool, one from Bradford and three from Manchester and Sheffield. Other services terminated at either Woodford Halse, Leicester or Nottingham.

The two crack trains at this time were the 'Master Cutler' and the 'South Yorkshireman'. Inaugurated in 1947 the 'Cutler' departed from

Below: **The former Great Central line left the 'cut-off' route just a few miles north of Princes Risborough at Ashendon Junction. On 26 July 1954 the 1.10pm service from Paddington to Chester passes the junction hauled by No 4977 Watcombe Hall (84C). The former GC line can be seen in the left background.** *S. Creer*

Above: **The 'Master Cutler' service to and from Sheffield was for many years the crack GC express. The up service, the 7.40am departure from Sheffield Victoria, hauled by Leicester (38C)-based 'V2' No 60854, stands after arrival at Marylebone on 28 September 1957.** *C. P. Boocock*

Below: **Colwick (38A)-based ex-Great Central Robinson Class A5 4-6-2T No 69801 stands at Marylebone on 5 April 1956 with the 11.20am service to High Wycombe. The 'A5' was temporarily back at Neasden for the 50th anniversary of the opening of the GW/GC joint line.** *J. D. Edwards*

Above: **In the days when the 'A3s' reigned supreme on GC services, Neasden (34E)-based No 60111** *Enterprise* **waits to depart from Marylebone on 10 April 1953 with the inaugural 'Starlight Special' overnight service to Glasgow St Enoch.** *Brian Morrison*

Right: **Ex-Great Western '4300' class Mogul 2-6-0 No 9311 from Southall (81C) stands at Marylebone with an engineers' special on a wet 28 October 1952 morning. No 9311 was later renumbered 7333 by the Western Region.** *Philip J. Kelley*

Left: **One of the many joint-line stopping services, the 12.20pm service to High Wycombe hauled by 'L1' 2-6-4T No 67796 (34E) waits at Marylebone on 16 May 1957.**
J. D. Edwards

Below left: **From 1 February 1958 the 'L1s' were gradually withdrawn from the local services and replaced by ex-LMS 2-6-4Ts. On 2 June 1959 the 6.38pm service to High Wycombe is in the hands of ex-LMS 2-6-4T No 42283.**
J. D. Edwards

Right: **Another 'L1', No 67748 (34E), simmers at Marylebone on 16 May 1957 after arriving with an up stopping service from Aylesbury.**
J. D. Edwards

Sheffield at 7.50am arriving at Marylebone at 11.24am; the return service left Marylebone at 6.18pm. The 'South Yorkshireman' service was inaugurated in 1948; the up service left Bradford Exchange at 10am and arrived at Marylebone some 5½hr later, the down service departing from Marylebone at 4.50pm. Depending on the loading, these services were worked using 'A3s', 'V2s' or even 'B1s' with locomotive and crew changes taking place at Leicester. Another interesting service was inaugurated in April 1953, this being the 'Starlight Special', an overnight service between Marylebone and Glasgow St Enoch. The cheap fares (£3.10s [£3.50] return) made the service very popular.

Suburban services from Marylebone to Aylesbury and Woodford were hauled by ex-Great Central 'A5' 4-6-2Ts and ex-LNER 'L1' 2-6-4Ts, as were the joint line services to High Wycombe and Princes Risborough, but sadly the 'A5s' were allocated away during 1954. 'L1s' were also used on the London Transport services from Baker Street to Aylesbury, taking over from London Transport Bo-Bo electric locomotives at Rickmansworth.

There was a considerable amount of freight traffic travelling to and from London including a daily Sheffield-Marylebone express freight, but because of the congestion over the Met section, particularly during the day, many of these services travelled via the joint line. Other services included a number of parcels and coal trains. The main freight shed on the southern section was at Woodford Halse, but freight services brought many different locomotives, including classes 'V2' 2-6-2s, 'B1' 4-6-0s, 'B16' 4-6-0s, 'K2' 2-6-0s, 'K3' 2-6-0s, ex-War Department 2-8-0s and BR Standard Class 9Fs, from other depots. Neasden

also had a number of Standard Class 4 2-6-0s for local freight and passenger work.

On 1 February 1958 the ex-Great Central lines were taken over by the London Midland Region and within a short space of time ex-LNER types became the exception rather than the rule. From the start of the summer timetable in 1958 the 'Master Cutler' service to and from Sheffield was switched to run from King's Cross. The few remaining 'A3s' had left the Great Central by the start of the winter 1957 timetable. They were initially replaced by 'V2s', but by 1960 these too were replaced by a number of ex-LMS Class 5 4-6-0s. The suburban services also underwent a change as the 'L1s' were replaced by a mixture of ex-LMS Stanier and Fairburn 2-6-4Ts together with BR Standard 2-6-4Ts.

London Midland control soon started to bite and from Saturday 2 January 1960 through weekday passenger services to Sheffield and Manchester, including the 'South Yorkshireman', were withdrawn leaving a basic timetable of just three daily semi-fast services to and from Nottingham together with a late night parcels and newspaper train to Manchester. However, electrification work on the ex-LNWR main line saw a number of parcels trains together with a sleeping car service to Manchester switched from Euston to Marylebone. Suburban services also saw quite a change when, in 1961, the first DMUs were introduced on some of the suburban services. On 11 September 1961 all services north of Amersham were taken over by the London Midland Region and Amersham became the terminus of the Metropolitan Line service from Baker Street. The line between Rickmansworth and Amersham had previously been electrified, with electric services commencing on

12 September 1960. The last steam passenger service from Rickmansworth took place on 9 September hauled by Fairburn 2-6-4T No 42070 and from Monday 11 September the ex-Metropolitan Bo-Bo electric locomotives were withdrawn from passenger services and replaced by A60 stock electric trains. The electrification work also included the Chalfont-Chesham branch. During the early and mid-1950s the branch was worked using ex-GC 'C13' class 4-4-2Ts, but these were replaced in the period just prior to electrification by ex-LMS Class 2 2-6-2Ts.

On 18 June 1962 all suburban services out of Marylebone were fully dieselised using newly-introduced DMUs. The last local steam-hauled train via the ex-GC main line was the 7.40pm to Aylesbury and Woodford and, on the following day (Sunday), the last steam local, the 5.20pm to Brackley, traversed the joint line. On 18 June 1962 the steam sheds at Neasden and Aylesbury were closed, Neasden's remaining steam turns being taken over by Cricklewood (14A). Interestingly, Neasden had retained an allocation of ex-LNER 'B1' 4-6-0s right up until closure. Services saw a further reduction when, from 4 March 1963, all local services north of Aylesbury were withdrawn resulting in the closure of a number of stations. By this date the Nottingham services were being operated using ex-LMS Class 5s, together with 'Britannias' and Standard Class 5s, along with a number of 'Royal Scots', many of which had seen better days. Looking through the *Railway Observer* magazine

during this period one reads seemingly endless reports of locomotive failures.

The remaining freight services at this time were in the hands of ex-LMS Class 5 4-6-0s and Class 8F 2-8-0s, together with Standard Class 5 4-6-0s and '9F' 2-10-0s, with the odd sprinkling of new diesel electrics but, from 14 June 1965, through freight services were withdrawn south of Leicester. Woodford Yard and Motive Power Depot were also closed on the same date. The closure of Leicester Central on 6 July 1964 now saw much of the motive power over the line supplied by either Annesley or, until its closure on 14 December 1964, Cricklewood. After this date servicing was switched to Willesden and when that depot was closed on 27 September 1965, incredibly it was Banbury that took over many of the GC duties. The shed gained a number of ex-LMS Class 5s and also eight 'Britannia' Pacifics for GC line services. The 'Britannias' were not a success and were replaced in January 1966 by more ex-LMS Class 5s. Steam services from Marylebone now comprised three up and three down services (two parcels and four passenger) to Nottingham. There was also an 8.45pm (SX) parcels service to York and a 10.45pm (SO) passenger service to Manchester. The rundown of the line became complete when, on 3 September 1966, the remaining through services north of Aylesbury were withdrawn. The last passenger train and also the last steam train, the 10.45pm (SO) service to Manchester was hauled out of Marylebone by ex-LMS Class 5 No 44984.

Below left: **Another shot shows the coaling area on 6 April 1957 with, from left to right, 'L1' No 67740 (34E), 'B1' No 61078 (38E) and 'L1' 67778 (34E).** *J. D. Edwards*

Right: **Rather than travel out to the main depot at Neasden between duties, engines were coaled, watered and turned in Marylebone yard. Standing on the turntable here on 31 July 1959 is ex-LNER 'V2' No 60831 from Leicester Central (15E).** *J. D. Edwards*

Centre right: **The 12.15pm service from Marylebone to Manchester, hauled by 'V2' 2-6-2 No 60831 (15E), climbs out of Marylebone on 31 July 1959. This service travelled via the ex-GC/GW joint line calling at High Wycombe before rejoining the GC route at Grendon Underwood Junction.** *J. D. Edwards*

Below: **A slightly higher viewpoint shows the approach to Marylebone and the position of the small loco yard on the right. On 24 July 1960 'V2' No 60856 from York (50A) departs with the 3.45pm stopping service to Nottingham. York-based 'V2s' were regular performers on this service.**
J. D. Edwards

Above: Class A3 4-6-2 No 60052 *Prince Palatine* (38C) winds its way into Marylebone on 12 May 1954 with the up 'Master Cutler' service. *Philip J. Kelley*

Left: Taken from the cab of an adjacent 'L1' arriving on a service from High Wycombe, ex-LNER 'B1' class 4-6-0 No 61028 *Umseke* (34E) is seen departing from Marylebone in the early 1950s with a down stopping service to Woodford Halse. *Peter Stears*

Below left: A rather run-down looking rebuilt 'Jubilee' class 4-6-0 No 45735 *Comet* from Annesley (16B) speeds through the north London suburb of Kilburn on 21 March 1964 with the 2.38pm service to Nottingham. An ex-GC driver once told me that in the last few years of GC main line services the general state of the motive power was a disgrace and an insult to the crews who had to try and keep time with them. *Brian Stephenson*

Above right: Wembley Stadium was situated on the section between Neasden Junction and Northolt, bringing many visiting locomotives to the line on football excursion traffic. On the occasion of a schoolboys' international game on 26 April 1958 modified 'Hall' class 4-6-0 No 6964 *Thornbridge Hall* (Shrewsbury [84G]) departs from Wembley Hill with the 6.53pm return excursion to Shrewsbury. *C. R. L. Coles*

Below right: Return excursions at Wembley Hill on the occasion of an international schoolboys' football match at Wembley on 30 March 1957. On the left is 'Hall' class 4-6-0 No 4949 *Packwood Hall* on a return excursion to its home base at Taunton and on the right is a King's Cross (34A) 'B1' 4-6-0 No 61394 on a return excursion to Doncaster and Newark. *C. R. L. Coles*

Above left: **This section of the line from Neasden Junction to Northolt was extremely costly to construct due in no small measure to the deep cutting at Wembley and the tunnel at Sudbury Hill. Here on 1 August 1960 the 1.10pm service from High Wycombe to Marylebone approaches Sudbury Hill tunnel hauled by ex-LMS 2-6-4T No 42092.** *J. D. Edwards*

Left: **Looking in the opposite direction on the same day, fellow class member No 42618 emerges from the tunnel with the 1.20pm service from Marylebone to High Wycombe.** *J. D. Edwards*

Above : **Another football excursion from Wembley to Weston-super-Mare hauled by 'Castle' class No 5023** *Brecon Castle* **(82C) climbs the sharp gradient at Neasden Junction on 29 April 1961. The service will reach GW metals via Acton Wells Junction.** *M. Pope*

Centre right: **The ex-Great Central steam depot was at Neasden. Standing in the yard in September 1955 is a Neasden (34E)-allocated 'B1' class 4-6-0 No 61009** *Hartebeeste.* **From 1948 the shed was coded '34E' but from 1 February 1958 it became part of the London Midland Region Cricklewood division, being coded '14D'.** *G. Wheeler*

Right: **Ex-Great Central Parker 'N5/2' 0-6-2T No 69315 (34E) stands in the yard at Neasden on 9 August 1955. The 'N5s' were used on both joint line and GC services to and from Aylesbury.** *Philip J. Kelley*

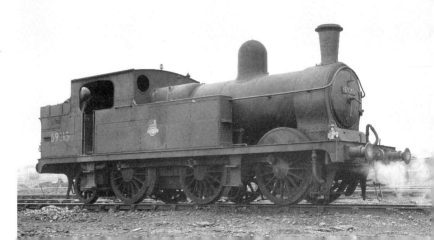

Above: **A view of the shed yard on 9 September 1961, with ex-LMS 2-6-4T Nos 42080, 42070, 42291 and 'Crab' 2-6-0 No 42747 present. The shed was closed on 18 June 1962.** *Hugh Ballantyne*

Below: **BR Standard Class 5 4-6-0 No 73159 stands outside the shed at Neasden on 1 June 1957. The locomotive is minus its shedcode plate, but was allocated to Neasden (34E) during the same month.** *R. C. Riley*

Above right: **The 2.38pm service from Marylebone to Nottingham Victoria hauled by 'Royal Scot' 4-6-0 No 46112 *Sherwood Forester* crosses the ex-LNWR main line at Kenton on 28 December 1963. Annesley had an allocation of nine 'Royal Scots' at this time especially for working the GC Services.** *R. L. Sewell*

Right: **Ex-LMS Class 5 No 45234 (14D)** runs past Moor Park on 3 June 1960 with a Nottingham-Marylebone service. On the left work has started on the Metropolitan Line modernisation which included the provision of a four-track layout between Harrow-on-the-Hill and Watford South Junction, the work being finished on 18 June 1962. *D. Trevor Rowe*

Below: **This second picture taken** from the same spot again on 3 June 1960 shows an up semi-fast service from Woodford to Marylebone hauled by 'B1' 4-6-0 No 61186 of **Woodford Halse (2F).** *D. Trevor Rowe*

Above: **Towards the end of steam services on the GC ex-LMS Class 5 4-6-0 No 44858 heads a morning Nottingham–Marylebone service near Moor Park on 24 August 1966. The electrified tracks on the right are the Metropolitan lines to Watford and Amersham.** *P. H. Groom*

Below: **A view of Northwood taken on a cold morning on 6 March 1965 as ex-LMS Class 5 No 45289 speeds by with the 8.15am service to Nottingham. This was the regular formation at this time — a Class 5 and four coaches.** *Courtney Haydon*

Above: **'A3' Pacific No 60104 *Solario* (38C) enters Rickmansworth on Saturday 10 September 1955 with the 3.20pm service from Marylebone to Manchester. Standing in the up platform is ex-Metropolitan Bo-Bo electric No 4 *Lord Byron* with the 3.56pm service to Baker Street.** *R. M. Newland*

Below: **Ex-LNER push-pull fitted 'N5' No 69257 (34E) prepares to depart from Rickmansworth on 9 February 1957 with a service to Aylesbury, whilst standing in the up platform is ex-Metropolitan Bo-Bo electric locomotive No 12 *Sarah Siddons* which has just brought the train in from Baker Street.** *J. D. Edwards*

Above: **Stanier 'Black 5' No 45114 from Banbury (2D) runs through Rickmansworth on 6 November 1965 with the 8.15am service from Nottingham Victoria to Marylebone.** *M. J. Fox*

Left: **The down 'South Yorkshireman', the 4.50pm service from Marylebone to Bradford, hauled by Heaton (52B)-allocated ex-LNER 'V2' 2-6-2 No 60846 speeds past Chorley Wood on 24 September 1959.** *J. D. Edwards*

Above right: **A view of the same location on 6 April 1963 shows ex-LMS Class 5 No 44665 from Annesley (16B) on the 2.38pm service from Marylebone to Nottingham. By this date there were only five through services a day using the ex-GC route.** *G. T. Robinson*

Right: **A rather different type of motive power as ex-SR 'Merchant Navy' class 4-6-2 No 35022 *Holland–America Line* climbs up through Chorley Wood on 27 November 1965 with a Warwickshire Railway Society special from Waterloo to Crewe via Acton Wells Junction, Rickmansworth, Bletchley and Nuneaton.** *R. L. Sewell*

Left: **On the same day the 4.8pm service from Chesham, hauled by fellow class member No 41272 (14D), passes through delightful countryside near Quill Hall.** *M. Yarwood*

Centre left: **Specially cleaned up for the occasion, ex-LMS Fairburn 2-6-4T No 42070 (14D) stands at Rickmansworth on 9 September 1961 with a farewell special on the last day of Metropolitan steam working between Rickmansworth and Aylesbury.** *Hugh Ballantyne*

Below left: **Ex-LMS 'Jubilee' 4-6-0 No 45709 *Implacable* from Saltley (21A) stands at Amersham on 26 May 1963 with a special service commemorating the centenary of the Metropolitan Railway. The train which ran to Aylesbury is formed of ex-Met steam stock.** *A. Swain*

Above right: **The down 'South Yorkshireman' service from Marylebone to Bradford approaches Wendover on 2 June 1952 double-headed by 'B1' No 61141 and 'A3' No 60103 *Flying Scotsman*. The 'A3' was allocated to Leicester Central (38C) during the early 1950s.** *J. Collier*

Below right: **The attractive station at Wendover is seen here on 13 April 1959 as ex-LMS Class 4 2-6-4T No 42283 (14D) arrives with an afternoon service from Baker Street to Aylesbury. Wendover was opened by the Metropolitan Railway on 1 September 1892.** *J. D. Edwards*

Above left: **The up 'South Yorkshireman', the 10am service from Bradford to Marylebone, speeds through Wendover station on 2 October 1959 hauled by ex-LNER 'B1' No 61106 (15E).** *J. D. Edwards*

Left: **Ex-LNER 'L1' class 2-6-4T No 67714 (34E) ascends the 1 in 117 bank soon after leaving Wendover station with the 1.13pm service from Aylesbury to Baker Street on 2 June 1952.** *J. Collier*

Above: **'B1' 4-6-0 No 61185 from Leicester Central departs from Aylesbury in June 1948 with the up 'South Yorkshireman' service, the 10am from Bradford Exchange to Marylebone.** *H. K. Harman*

Below: **Ex-GW '5100' class No 5152 (84C) and autocoach *Thrush* wait at Aylesbury Town in the early 1960s with the auto-service to Princes Risborough and Banbury.** *R. H. G. Simpson*

Above left: **BR Standard Class 4 2-6-4T No 80143 (34E) departs from Aylesbury with an up stopping service to Baker Street on 19 April 1957. From 1956 Neasden had an allocation of 10 of these Standard 2-6-4Ts, initially replacing a number of the older 'L1' class 2-6-4Ts on ex-Great Central, Metropolitan and Joint Line suburban services. They were themselves replaced by ex-LMS Class 4 2-6-4Ts during 1959.** *R. C. Riley*

Centre left: **An interesting shot of ex-Metropolitan 'E' class 0-4-4T No L46 as it departs from Aylesbury with ECS on 11 August 1956. The locomotive was used at this time mainly on ballast trains, but on this occasion was being tested on passenger trains prior to working a railtour.** *R. C. Riley*

Below left: **Neasden (34E)-allocated 'A3' Pacific No 60051** *Blink Bonny* **prepares to depart from Aylesbury Town on 5 May 1953 with the 10am semi-fast service from Marylebone to Manchester. The first station on this site was opened by the Wycombe Railway on 1 October 1863. It was rebuilt during 1908 to accommodate the Metropolitan Railway services, and in 1925 a new bay was added with the platforms extended to cope with longer trains.** *L. G. Skidmore*

Right: **Fellow class member No 60049** *Galtee More* **(Leicester [38C]) departs from Aylesbury with the up 'South Yorkshireman' on 21 September 1954. I can well remember spending over an hour on the footplate of this locomotive at Banbury in 1956 as it waited to work the Sundays-only service from Banbury to Woodford and Leicester.** *L. V. Reason*

The 2.30pm arrival at Aylesbury from Princes Risborough is hauled by ex-LNER 'N5' 0-6-2T No 69259 (34E) on 23 August 1950. At the top left part of the small sub shed can be seen. *E. C. Griffith*

Left: **The 7.20pm service from Quainton Road to Marylebone hauled by 'L1' No 67767 (34E) waits at Aylesbury on 23 June 1958.** *M. Mitchell*

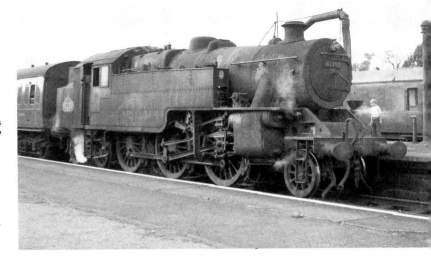

Below left: **Another 1950s view shows 'L1' No 67753 (34E) leaving Aylesbury with the 1.9pm Metropolitan Line service to Baker Street. The 'L1' will be replaced at Rickmansworth with an ex-Metropolitan Bo-Bo electric locomotive.** *Ian Allan Library*

Above right: **Ex-LMS Fairburn Class 4 2-6-4T No 42282 (14D) stands at Aylesbury on 22 July 1961 with the 5.35pm stopping service to Marylebone.** *Courtney Haydon*

Centre right: **On the same day the 4.46pm service to Marylebone waits to depart hauled by Woodford Halse (2F)-allocated ex-LNER 'K3' class 2-6-0 No 61913. Although under Midland Region control, Woodford had no less than 11 examples of the class at this time.** *Courtney Haydon*

Below: **During the last few years of ex-Great Central through workings the services were in the hands of a variety of ex-LMS types. Looking down from the footbridge, ex-LMS 'Royal Scot' No 46112 *Sherwood Forester* from Annesley (16B) brings the 12.38pm Marylebone–Nottingham service into Aylesbury on 31 October 1962.** *Ian Allan Library*

Above: **Another member of the class, No 46122 *Royal Ulster Rifleman* (16B), takes water at Aylesbury prior to departing with the 2.38pm service to Nottingham on 28 May 1964. At this time the Marylebone–Nottingham services were the last rostered express duties for these locomotives.**
A. W. Smith

Below: **A view of Aylesbury Town shed in 1960 shows two Neasden engines, 2-6-4T No 42157 and 2-6-2T No 41329. The shed, which was sub to both Neasden and Slough, was closed to steam on 16 June 1962.**
Photomatic

Above right: **Ex-LMS 'Jubilee' class 4-6-0 No 45709 *Implacable* (Saltley [21A]) stands at the down platform at Aylesbury on 26 May 1963 with the return Metropolitan 'Jubilee' special to Baker Street. Notice the locomotive shed on the left being used at this time as a DMU stabling point.** *Courtney Haydon*

Below right: **A rather tired-looking 'Britannia' No 70046 *Anzac* (2D) pulls into Aylesbury in the autumn of 1965 with a service from Nottingham. Eight members of the class were allocated to Banbury (2D) in 1965 for use on GC services.** *D. Tuck*

Left: **On a frosty 24 January 1959 'V2' No 60879 (15E) approaches Aylesbury with the 7.40am service from Sheffield.** *M. Mitchell*

Above: **During the 1950s many of the ex-GC services were hauled by 'A3', 'V2' and 'B1' locomotives but occasionally ex-LNER 'K3' class 2-6-0s were also used. On 19 July 1958 No 61838 (Woodford [2F]) departs across the Vale of Aylesbury with the 5pm stopping service from Marylebone to Woodford Halse.** *M. Mitchell*

Below: **This picture would make an interesting 'then' and 'now' view as ex-LMS Class 5 No 44920 speeds through Quainton Road station with the 2.38pm service to Nottingham on 22 June 1966. The station now forms part of the Buckinghamshire Railway Centre. On the right is the old Brill branch platform.** *Courtney Haydon*

Left: **Great Central services that ran via the GW/GC joint line left the GC main line at Grendon Underwood Junction. The 6.18pm service from Marylebone to Sheffield hauled by 'B1' No 61206 (14D) is pictured here between Akeman Street and Grendon Underwood Junction on 2 July 1959.** *M. Mitchell*

Below left: **Another 'B1', No 61369 (15E), approaches Grendon Underwood Junction on 23 May 1959 with the up 10am 'South Yorkshireman' service from Bradford to Marylebone. The only two stations on the connecting line, at Akeman Street and Wotton, were closed on 7 July 1930 and 7 December 1953 respectively.** *M. Mitchell*

Above right: **Great Central services connected with the GW/GC joint line at Ashendon Junction. Here on 27 August 1955 'V2' No 60863 (38C) passes under the flying junction with the 11.22am (SO) service from Sheffield Victoria to Marylebone. The girder bridge carried the ex-GW 'cut-off' line to Birmingham over the GC line at this point.** *S. Creer*

Centre right: **Another shot of Ashendon Junction on 26 July 1954 as 'B1' No 61185 (38C) takes the GC route with the 11.55am (SO) service from Marylebone to Nottingham. Ashendon Junction signalbox (opened 21 March 1904) can just be seen on the left. The section from Ashendon to Grendon Underwood was closed on 3 September 1966.** *S. Creer*

Below: **The down 'Master Cutler' service approaches Quainton Road station in the early 1950s hauled by 'A3' Pacific No 60052 *Prince Palatine*. This was one of eight 'A3s' that at this time were based at Leicester Central (38C).** *Rev R. F. H. Hine*

Left: **North of Quainton, stations on the Great Central's London Extension were built as island platforms. This is shown to good effect at Calvert pictured here on 11 May 1964 as York (50A)-allocated 'V2' No 60831 speeds through the closed station at Calvert with the 2.38pm service to Nottingham. The wagons on the right are for the adjacent brickworks. Calvert station was closed to passengers on 4 March 1963. Today the brickworks are closed and the line is used by waste trains from Bath and London, the household waste being used to infill the adjacent quarry.** *M. Mensing*

Above: **Probably the most famous 'A3' of all, No 60103 *Flying Scotsman* (38C), speeds under the roadbridge at Quainton Road with the down 'South Yorkshireman', again in the early 1950s. Quainton Road was closed to passengers on 4 March 1963 but has since been reopened as part of the Buckinghamshire Railway Centre. Interestingly, the cracks on the roadbridge are still in evidence today.** *Rev R. F. H. Hine*

Left: **On 23 May 1954 the *Railway World* magazine ran an excursion to Quainton Road and Verney Junction using ex-Metropolitan 0-4-2T No L48. The train is pictured here during a photostop at Quainton Road.** *R. H. G. Simpson*

Above: **I have selected Brackley Central as the northern extremity of the ex-Great Central line covered in this book. This fine view of the station area shows a Leicester (15E)-allocated ex-LNER 'V2' class 2-6-0 No 60879 speeding through the station with the down 'South Yorkshireman' service on 4 July 1959. The 756ft-long viaduct across the Ouse valley is just obscured by the smoke from the locomotive.** *M. Mitchell*

Below: **An ex-LMS Class 5, No 44825 from Annesley (16B), heads a three-coach semi-fast service from Marylebone to Nottingham into Brackley on Saturday 19 March 1966. Already the goods yard has been lifted. The station and the line were closed on 3 September 1966.** *A. Muckley*

Above: **On 1 September 1966 and just two days before the end of through services from Marylebone, Class 5 No 45493 from Banbury (2D) stands at Marylebone with the 2.38pm service to Nottingham.** *J. H. Bird*

Below: **Again taken on the same day, Class 5 No 44840 (Banbury [2D]) stands at Aylesbury Town on the 4.38pm service from Marylebone to Nottingham.** *Ken Fairey*

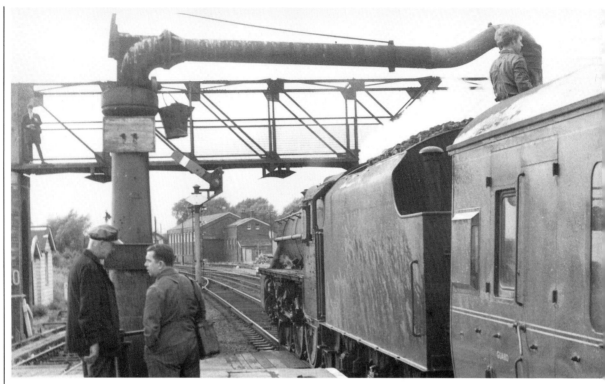

Above: **Another view of No 44840 at Aylesbury on the 4.38pm service to Nottingham. Whilst the fireman deals with the water crane, the driver is probably discussing the imminent end of both steam traction and through services over the line.** *Ken Fairey*

Below: **The penultimate 4.38pm service from Marylebone to Nottingham hauled by Class 5 No 44872 from Aston (2J) climbs the bank near Chorley Wood on 2 September 1966.** *R. L. Sewell*

Above: **The very last through service to Nottingham, the 4.38pm from Marylebone, hauled by Class 5 No 45292 from Tyseley (2A) eases its way through Harrow-on-the-Hill on 3 September 1966. The chalk inscription on the smokebox reads 'The Last Day Great Central'.** *B. H. Jackson*

Below: **The final picture in the GC section is of the last steam — and also last through — service to depart from Marylebone. Again on 3 September 1966 a rather worn out Class 5 No 44984 from Annesley (16B) waits to depart with the 10.45pm service to Manchester.** *E. J. S. Gadsden*

3. The GC/GW Joint Line Services and Motive Power

Probably the greatest variety in both services and motive power was to be seen over the joint line and 'cut-off' route. During the 1950s the main ex-GW services over the route comprised Paddington-Birmingham, Wolverhampton and Birkenhead trains. In the mid-1950s there was a two-hour interval service to and from Birkenhead. These services were still at this time in the hands of 'King' class locomotives which had been introduced on the line way back in 1928. Although the principal allocation was centred at Old Oak Common, Wolverhampton Stafford Road generally had an allocation of six. The crack train over the route was undoubtedly the 'Inter City', the 9am relief restaurant-car service to Wolverhampton, so named in October 1950. Motive power was usually provided by a 'King' class locomotive supplied by Old Oak Common for both the up and down services. A schedule of just two hours to cover the 110 miles, which

included a stop at High Wycombe, required some hard work from both the locomotive and crew. Another named train, the 'Cambrian Coast Express' 10.10am service from Paddington to Aberystwyth, ran nonstop from Paddington to Banbury covering the $67\frac{1}{2}$ miles in just 72min. Intermediate services were generally in the hands of 'Castle', 'Hall' and 'Grange' class 4-6-0s with the occasional '4300' class 2-6-0. Freight services brought an assortment of ex-Great Western types over the line including '2800' class 2-8-0s, '2251' class 0-6-0s and '5700' class 0-6-0PTs. Other

Below: **Ex-Great Western main line services over the joint line departed from Paddington. Here on 15 July 1957 'King' class No 6006** *King George I* **(84A) stands at platform No 1 with the 2.10pm departure for Birkenhead. On the left at platform No 2 an unidentified 'Britannia' prepares to depart with the 1.55pm service to Pembroke Dock.** *J. D. Edwards*

types included ex-WD 2-8-0s and BR Standard Class 9F 2-10-0s. Many of these trains carried perishables such as fruit and meat — in fact the evening meat train from Birkenhead to Paddington was a feature of the line for over 40 years and became a regular turn for the large Churchward '4700' class 2-8-0s.

Interwoven with these were the ex-Great Central services which also used the joint line. At various times during the 1950s both the 'Master Cutler' and 'South Yorkshireman' services to Sheffield and Bradford ran via the joint line. Another regular service was the 12.15pm from Marylebone to Manchester which called *en route* at High Wycombe. As already mentioned, ex-GC freight services from Woodford and beyond to London also used the route to avoid congestion on the Met section. These brought a succession of 'V2', 'B1', 'B16', 'K3', 'O1/4' 2-8-0s, ex-WD

2-8-0s and Standard Class 9F 2-10-0s. During the 1950s and early 1960s up to 12 goods and parcels trains were running each way daily on the ex-GC main line by way of Ashendon Junction.

Ex-Great Western passenger services over the 'cut-off' section to Banbury comprised semi-fast trains from Paddington to Banbury and Birmingham, and local services from Banbury to Princes Risborough and High Wycombe. These latter services together with the Princes Risborough-Aylesbury service were operated on the auto-train principle using ex-GW '4800' 0-4-2Ts and '5400/6400' auto-fitted 0-6-0PTs.

Bicester North, the main intermediate station over the Risborough-Banbury section, was also served until September 1960 by a slip coach from the 5.10pm fast service to Wolverhampton, which was then attached here to a semi-fast service to Birmingham.

Above left: **On 10 September 1960 another 'King', No 6005 *King George II* (84A) passes Subway Junction with the 1.10pm service to Wolverhampton. At this time the Western Region was running a one-hour interval service to Birmingham over the joint line.** *R. C. Riley*

Below left: **Looking down from the bridge at North Acton on 18 August 1953, modified 'Hall' class No 6966 *Witchingham Hall* (84C) takes the low level West London line with the 10.10am service from Birmingham Snow Hill to Margate. The remains of the Great Western station (closed 30 June 1947) can just be seen on the right.** *Ian Allan Library*

Above right: **Ex-LNER 'A3' class 4-6-2 No 60049 *Galtee More* (38C) speeds away over the ex-GC line at Northolt Junction *en route* to Wembley with an up Cup Final special from Manchester on 4 May 1957. No 60049 was withdrawn from ex-GC services just four months later, being allocated away to Grantham in September 1957.** *R. C. Riley*

Below right: **A return Cup Final special from Wembley to Manchester, hauled by an ex-LNER 'B1' class 4-6-0 No 61152 from Sheffield Darnall (41A), approaches Northolt Junction on 4 May 1957. The train is on the down ex-GC line at this point having just passed under the ex-Great Western main line. On the right is the LT Central Line extension to West Ruislip.** *R. C. Riley*

South of Princes Risborough suburban services reflected the joint ownership of the line, with a regular service from Marylebone to High Wycombe with some services running through to Princes Risborough and Aylesbury. These were operated during the 1950s by 'A5' 4-6-2T and 'L1' 2-6-4T locomotives. As already mentioned, the 'A5s' left in 1954 and, with the takeover of the ex-GC suburban services by the London Midland Region in February 1958, the ex-LNER 'L1s' were replaced by Stanier and Fairburn 2-6-4Ts and the newer Standard Class 4 2-6-4Ts.

In January 1960 joint line traffic was reduced with the withdrawal of the through services between Marylebone, Manchester and Sheffield but this was more than compensated for with the introduction, by the Western Region, of a one-hour interval service between Paddington, Birmingham and Wolverhampton. This was to counter the reduction in services to and from Euston due to electrification work over the ex-LNWR line. The new service provided 15 down and 14 up trains daily, many of them strengthened to 12- and 14-coach formations. Throughout this period the 'Kings' continued to perform admirably. In order to operate the service Stafford Road's 'King' allocation rose to 12 and there were also 16 at Old Oak Common. During 1962 several of the new Type 4 'Western' class diesel-hydraulics were introduced on to the services and on 10 September 1962 the remaining 'Kings' were withdrawn *en bloc* and replaced by the new Type 4s.

During April 1961 DMUs had started to appear on some of the Maidenhead-Aylesbury workings. On 16 June 1962 the '4800' class 0-4-2Ts left the area when the Banbury auto-trains were withdrawn and replaced by single-car diesel-units. On the same day the Princes Risborough-Aylesbury auto workings were also replaced by DMUs with the Marylebone-Princes Risborough service being extended to run through to Aylesbury and from Monday 18 June 1962 all joint line suburban services from Marylebone were operated by DMUs. Interestingly, the single-car Banbury working was itself withdrawn on 7 January 1963 and all intermediate stations on the 'cut-off' route north of Princes Risborough (with the exception of Bicester North) were closed. Steam finally disappeared from passenger services over the joint line when, on 11 June 1965, the last regular steam working, the 4.15pm service from Paddington to Banbury, was hauled by 'Castle' class No 7029 *Clun Castle*. This was also the last scheduled steam working from Paddington. Some freight and parcels services including the Marylebone-Nottingham newspaper train and the Woodford-Neasden (house coal) train remained steam-operated right up until December 1965.

Below: **BR Standard Class 2 2-6-4T No 80141 (34E) climbs away from South Ruislip on 4 May 1957 with the 6.22pm service from Princes Risborough to Marylebone. The station and junction can just be seen in the background.** *R. C. Riley*

Above: **Ex-Great Western 'Castle' class 4-6-0 No 5010** *Restormel Castle* **(84A) speeds through South Ruislip on 4 May 1957 with an up Cup Final special from Birmingham to Wembley.** *R. C. Riley*

Below: **Unusual motive power for the 11.10am service from Paddington to Wolverhampton is 'Britannia' No 70020** *Mercury* **(81A) seen here approaching South Ruislip station in February 1952. The 'Britannias' were tried on these services soon after delivery to the Western Region but were not a success and were soon removed.** *C. R. L. Coles*

Above: **Back on its old stamping ground once again, preserved Class A3 No 4472** *Flying Scotsman* **speeds through West Ruislip on 20 April 1963 with a Festiniog Railway special from Paddington. The locomotive as No 60103 was allocated to Leicester Central in the early 1950s.** *C. R. L. Coles*

Left: **Ex-WD 'Austerity' class 2-8-0 No 90516 from Woodford Halse (2F) accelerates away through West Ruislip on 2 March 1963 with a return empty coal train from Neasden to Woodford Yard.** *Courtney Haydon*

Below: **The joint line was regularly used each year for football specials travelling to and from Wembley. On 4 May 1963 an up Cup Final special from Leicester passes West Ruislip. The train is hauled by 'Jubilee' class 4-6-0 No 45598** *Basutoland* **from Burton (17B). For the record, Manchester United beat Leicester City 3-1.** *C. R. L. Coles*

Right: **A return Cup Final special from Wembley to Leicester hauled by a Sheffield Darnall-allocated 'B1' No 61316 speeds over the water troughs at West Ruislip on 4 May 1963.** *Peter Stears*

Below: **A down stopping service from Marylebone to High Wycombe hauled by BR Standard Class 4 2-6-0 No 76041 (of Neasden [34E]) enters the cutting at Harefield in September 1954. Ten of these Standard Class 4s were allocated to Neasden during the 1950s and were used on both passenger and goods services.** *Real Photos*

Right: **Another shot taken at Harefield on 12 May 1951 shows a rather grubby 'King' No 6004 *King George III* (of Stafford Road [84A]) on a heavily loaded 2.10pm service to Birkenhead. This service ran nonstop to Banbury covering the 67½ miles in just 71min.** *E. R. Wethersett*

Left: **A fine portrait of the 7.30am service from Shrewsbury to Paddington hauled by 'King' No 6004** *King George III* **(84A) as it speeds through South Harefield cutting on 12 May 1951. South Harefield Halt which was closed on 30 September 1931, was situated just behind the overbridge.** *E. R. Wethersett*

Below left: **Denham Golf Club Platform, as its name implies, was opened by the GWR on 22 July 1912 to serve the nearby golf club. The 'Platform' suffix was dropped by the Western Region on 20 September 1954. The station, which is still open, is seen here on 10 March 1956 as 'L1' No 67794 (34E) arrives with an up stopping service from High Wycombe to Marylebone.** *M. Yarwood*

Above right: **A view from the down platform at Denham Golf Club as a rather smoky ex-LMS Fairburn 2-6-4T pulls in on 7 April 1960 with a Marylebone-High Wycombe service.** *Peter Stears*

Centre right: **King's Cross (34A)-allocated Gresley 'A4' Pacific No 60014** *Silver Link* **makes a fine sight as it speeds past Denham Golf Club Platform on 12 May 1956 with the 'Ian Allan** *Trains Illustrated* **Pennine Pullman'. The special ran from Marylebone to Sheffield and Todmorden, returning to King's Cross via the East Coast main line. The fare, just 55 shillings.** *Philip J. Kelley*

Below right: **In 1953 Neasden (34E) had an allocation of nine Ivatt Class 4 2-6-0s which were used on local stopping services on both the GC main and GC/GW joint lines. Pictured here on 11 April 1953 No 43127 heads the 11.20am service from Marylebone to Princes Risborough near Denham. These locomotives were replaced at Neasden during 1954 with 10 new Standard Class 4 2-6-0s.** *Brian Morrison*

Left: **An Up Cup final special from Leicester to Wembley hauled by ex-LNER 'B1' No 61154 from Sheffield Darnall (41A) approaches Denham Golf Club on 5 May 1961. For the record, Tottenham beat Leicester 2-0.** *D. Trevor Rowe*

Below left: **Looking in the opposite direction on the same day, an ex-GW 'County' class 4-6-0 No 1018 *County of Leicester* (84A) approaches the camera with the 11.30am service from Oxford to Paddington via Thame and Princes Risborough. These locomotives were not regular performers over the joint section.** *Brian Morrison*

Above right: **A down goods hauled by '2251' class 0-6-0 No 3216 (84C) passes through the cutting at Denham on 11 April 1953. The 0-6-0s were generally used over the joint line on pick-up goods services, calling at the various stations and yards *en route* between Banbury and Acton.** *Brian Morrison*

Centre right: **Again on 11 April 1953 an ex-WD class 2-8-0, No 90485 (81C) minus smokebox numberplate, plods through Denham with some down coal empties for Woodford yard. Ugly they may have been, but these locomotives were a mainstay of freight traffic in this country from the end of World War 2 right up to the end of steam traction.** *Brian Morrison*

Right: **'Hall' class 4-6-0 No 5996 *Mytton Hall* (81A) speeds through a rather wet Gerrards Cross with a down excursion comprising mostly ex-LMS stock on 27 July 1957. The cutting here is over 1½ miles long and 85ft deep in places and during the construction of this section of the line over 1,228cu tons of chalk were removed.** *J. F. Loader*

Left: **The depth of the cutting at Gerrards Cross can be seen to good effect in this shot of ex-LMS Class 4 2-6-4T No 42230 (34E) arriving with an up stopping service from Princes Risborough on 5 May 1961. Notice that the station entrance is built on two levels. Today the two up tracks have been removed and the up platform has been extended outward, the down main becoming the up line.** *D. Trevor Rowe*

Below left: **Looking down from the roadbridge to the north of Gerrards Cross on 5 May 1961 modified 'Hall' class No 7908 *Henshall Hall* from Tyseley (84E) pilots 'King' class No 6022 *King Edward III* (84A) through the station with the 1.10pm service from Paddington to Wolverhampton.** *D. Trevor Rowe*

Above right: **'Castle' No 5060 *Earl of Berkeley* speeds through Gerrards Cross on 6 June 1951 with 'The William Shakespeare', the 10.10am service from Paddington to Wolverhampton. The service was inaugurated for the 1951 Festival of Britain and carried through coaches for Stratford-upon-Avon, hence the name.** *Great Western Trust*

Centre right: **A low-level view of 'King' No 6018 *King Henry V1* (81A) as it speeds through Seer Green & Jordans station with the 11.43am Birkenhead-Paddington service on 5 July 1952. Seer Green & Jordans was opened as Beaconsfield Golf Links Halt on 1 January 1915, being renamed as Seer Green on 16 December 1918.** *Brian Morrison*

Right: **At this point the up line is on a falling gradient for a distance of about seven miles down to Denham, which made for some fast running. On 5 July 1952 Thompson 'B1' 4-6-0 No 61376 from Gorton (38A) speeds through the cutting near Seer Green with an excursion to Marylebone. The headboard reads 'Bentley-Annual Outing'.** *Brian Morrison*

Left: **An up mixed freight hauled by a Southall (81C)-allocated ex-GW '4300' class 2-6-0 No 6300 passes through Seer Green cutting on 5 July 1952. The locomotive is fitted with one of the intermediate type tenders.** *Brian Morrison*

Centre left: **Another shot taken near Seer Green on 5 July 1952 shows a rather grubby Wolverhampton Stafford Road (84A) 'King' No 6005 *King George II* on the 2.10pm service from Paddington to Wolverhampton and Birkenhead.** *Brian Morrison*

Below: **Usually the heavier services from Paddington to Birkenhead were hauled by 'King' class engines but, on 3 March 1957, the 2.10pm service to Birkenhead, comprising 11 coaches, speeds through Seer Green hauled by 'Castle' No 5056 *Earl of Powis* (81A). When in top condition the 'Castles' had little trouble with these loads over the 'cut-off' route.** *J. D. Edwards*

Above right: **The 6.45am service from Wolverhampton to Paddington, hauled by 'King' class 4-6-0 No 6004 *King George III* (84A), speeds through the delightful Buckinghamshire countryside near Beaconsfield on 5 July 1952.** *Brian Morrison*

Below right: **Sporting its brass bell, 'King' No 6000 *King George V* (81A) unusually takes the platform line at Beaconsfield on 21 April 1957 with the 11.10am service from Paddington to Birkenhead. The service ran nonstop to Banbury and was apparently diverted due to a freight blocking the through road.** *J. D. Edwards*

Above left: **Many of the freights over the joint route were hauled by ex-WD 2-8-0s. On 2 April 1958 Southall (81C)-based No 90207 passes through Beaconsfield with some down coal empties, possibly for Woodford Yard.** *J. D. Edwards*

Left: **Yet another 'King', No 6020 King Henry IV (84A) on an up service from Birkenhead to Paddington, passes '2884' class 2-8-0 No 3819 at Beaconsfield on 21 April 1957.** *J. D. Edwards*

Above: **Looking down from the edge of the embankment at Beaconsfield on 30 July 1960, ex-LMS Class 5 No 44753 from Leeds (55A), fitted with Caprotti valve gear and Timpken roller bearings, passes through with a down empty stock train from Marylebone. Most extra services from Marylebone used the joint line section.** *K. L. Cook*

Right: **Joint line notice at Beaconsfield, April 1958.** *J. D. Edwards*

For a number of years the ex-LNER 'L1' class 2-6-4Ts formed the main motive power for the joint line services from Marylebone to High Wycombe, Princes Risborough and Aylesbury. On 2 April 1958 the 11.20am service from Marylebone to High Wycombe prepares to depart from Beaconsfield hauled by 'L1' No 67778. From 1 February 1958 these services were taken over by the London Midland Region who eventually replaced the 'L1s' with ex-LMS 2-6-4Ts. *J. D. Edwards*

Above: **The new order pictured here in June 1961 as ex-LMS 2-6-4T No 42629 (14D) arrives with the 1.20pm stopping service from Marylebone to Princes Risborough. From 18 June 1962 steam traction on the local services from Marylebone to Princes Risborough was withdrawn and services were operated using DMUs.** *W. Turner*

Centre left: **Another photograph taken in June 1961 shows Banbury (84C)-allocated BR Standard Class 9F 2-10-0 No 92207 running through with a freight from Oxley to Acton yard.** *W. Turner*

Below left: **'King' class 4-6-0 No 6028 *King George VI* (81A) blasts its way out of the 348yd-long White House Farm tunnel, between Beaconsfield and High Wycombe, on 18 March 1957 with the down 'Inter-City', the 9am service from Paddington to Wolverhampton.** *J. D. Edwards*

Above right: **'Castle' class No 7029 *Clun Castle* approaches White House Farm tunnel on 3 April 1965 with a Warwickshire Railway Society special from Birmingham to Swindon Works. The train travelled via the joint line and the Greenford Loop.** *H. K. Harman*

Below right: **Stafford Road (Wolverhampton)-allocated 'Castle' No 5031 *Totnes Castle* approaches High Wycombe on 6 June 1953 with the 7.30am relief service from Shrewsbury to Paddington.** *Brian Morrison*

Left: **The 9.25pm service from Glasgow Central to Kensington Olympia, diverted to Marylebone, departs from High Wycombe on 27 July 1963 behind Crewe North (5A)-allocated ex-LMS rebuilt 'Patriot' class 4-6-0 No 45534 *E. Tootal Broadhurst*. The train is on the down line due to single line working between High Wycombe and Beaconsfield.** *H. K. Harman*

Bottom left: **The up 'Inter-City' 4.35pm service from Wolverhampton (Low Level) restarts its journey from High Wycombe on 23 September 1954. The service, which was normally a 'King' turn, is unusually hauled by Castle No 5031 *Totnes Castle* (84A).** *E. R. Wethersett*

Above right: **Brighton-allocated ex-LBSCR Class H2 4-4-2 No 32425 *Trevose Head* stands at High Wycombe on 29 July 1956 with the 'Riverside Special', a ramblers' excursion from East Croydon to Marlow. The train reversed at High Wycombe and returned via Maidenhead.** *M. Yarwood*

Centre right: **An up Cup Final special taking Leicester City fans to Wembley makes its way through High Wycombe on 4 May 1963 hauled by ex-LMS Royal Scot class 4-6-0 No 46160 *Queen Victoria's Rifleman*.** *Peter Stears*

Below right: **The large Churchward '4700' class 2-8-0s were regular performers over the joint line. Here on 13 April 1962 No 4700 stands at High Wycombe with the 11.5am Banbury-Old Oak Common mixed freight.** *Peter Stears*

Left: **Reflecting once again that this was a joint line, 'L1' No 67756 stands in the bay platform at High Wycombe on 5 April 1957 with the 12.10pm service to Marylebone.**
J. D. Edwards

Centre left: **Looking from the down platform at High Wycombe on 17 September 1962 BR Standard Class 9F No 92220 *Evening Star* runs through with a Banbury Yard-Old Oak Common freight service. At this time the locomotive was allocated to Oxford (81F) and was generally used on car trains from Morris Cowley to Washwood Heath.** *H. K. Harman*

Below left: **Ex-LNER 'B1' class 4-6-0 No 61167 from Mexborough (41F) coasts through High Wycombe on 11 September 1961 with an excursion from Mexborough on the occasion of a women's hockey match at Wembley. The excursion terminated at Marylebone (for those not of a sporting nature?).** *H. K. Harman*

Above right: **Looking from the same spot as 'Castle' class No 5047 *Earl of Dartmouth* passes through on 14 October 1958 with the 6.30am service from Birkenhead to Paddington.** *H. K. Harman*

Below right: **'King' class 4-6-0 No 6005 *King George II* (84A) winds its way through High Wycombe on 10 November 1958 with the 7.30am service from Shrewsbury to Paddington.** *H. K. Harman*

Left: **On 11 March 1961 Class 'V2' No 60890 (2F) speeds through with another women's hockey match special from Rugby to Marylebone.** *H. K. Harman*

Below left: **For many years the 12.15pm service from Marylebone to Manchester ran via the joint line calling at High Wycombe. In March 1949 'A3' Pacific No 60053** *Sansovino,* **from New England depot, Peterborough, pulls away from the station and through the cutting** *en route* **to Manchester.** *H. K. Harman*

Right: **Another shot of the same service, taken on 23 May 1957, this time hauled by Leicester (38C)-based ex-LNER 'A3' 4-6-2 No 60104** *Solario.* **The 'A3' Pacifics were withdrawn from ex-Great Central services from 21 September 1957.** *J. D. Edwards*

Centre right: **The steam railway was worked by men who loved the job. Here, in 1963, a group of High Wycombe men pose for the camera in front of '6100' class No 6163. From left to right, drivers Tom Worley and John Bloxham, guard Gerry Churchward, foreman Dennis King and shunter Jim Sarney.** *Peter Stears*

Below: **The down 'Inter-City' 9am service from Paddington to Wolverhampton hauled by 'King' No 6009** *King Charles II* **(81A) crosses the Hughenden Road bridge on its way out of High Wycombe on 11 April 1957.** *J. D. Edwards*

Above left: **An up Schoolboy's International special from Nottingham Victoria to Wembley Hill hauled by ex-LMS Class 5 No 44941 (17B) approaches High Wycombe Middle box on 27 April 1965.**
H. K. Harman

Left: **Taken from the footplate of a '5700' class 0-6-0, another special taking fans to the 1963 Cup Final passes through Wycombe on 4 May 1963 hauled by a 'Royal Scot', No 46133** *The Green Howards.*
Peter Stears

Above: **This rather scenic shot shows an unidentified 'King' as it threads its way through High Wycombe on 30 June 1961 with the 2.10pm service from Paddington to Birkenhead. In the foreground is Wycombe North signalbox which was closed on 17 October 1976.**
D. Chipchase

Right: **'6100' class 2-6-2T No 6123 (Slough [81B]) departs from High Wycombe on 6 June 1953 with a local stopping service to Banbury (although the lamps suggest otherwise, as the photographer points out).** *Brian Morrison*

Above: **The same location but from a different angle shows ex-LNER 'B1' No 61158 from Doncaster (36A) with the 12.32pm cross-country service from Hastings to Manchester Piccadilly on 27 July 1963.**
Gerald T. Robinson

Left: **Neasden-allocated ex-LNER 'A5/1' 4-6-2T No 69814 passes West Wycombe yard with the 11.20am service from Marylebone to Princes Risborough on 6 June 1953. The 'A5s' were removed from these services early in 1954.**
Brian Morrison

Left: **Another of the services that used the joint line was the 2.32am Marylebone-Nottingham newspaper train. On 9 October 1965 BR Standard 'Britannia' class Pacific No 70054 *Dornoch Firth* from Banbury (2D) approaches High Wycombe with the return 11.15am Nottingham-Neasden ECS.**
H. K. Harman

Above: **Enthusiasts wave to the camera as 'Castle' class 4-6-0 No 7029 *Clun Castle* crosses the Bradenham Road Bridge at West Wycombe on 11 June 1965 with the 4.15pm service from Paddington to Banbury — the last booked steam-hauled service from Paddington.** *H. K. Harman*

Below: **'6100' class 2-6-2T No 6115 departs from West Wycombe on 12 May 1958 with the 3.43pm stopping service from High Wycombe to Aylesbury. The station here saw little custom and was closed by the Western Region on 3 November 1958.** *J. D. Edwards*

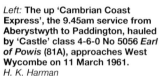

Left: **The up 'Cambrian Coast Express', the 9.45am service from Aberystwyth to Paddington, hauled by 'Castle' class 4-6-0 No 5056** *Earl of Powis* **(81A), approaches West Wycombe on 11 March 1961.** *H. K. Harman*

Centre left: **From High Wycombe the line climbed continuously for the next five miles up through the Chilterns to Saunderton. The bank made an excellent location for photography. On 2 October 1959 '6100' class 2-6-2T No 6115 makes its way up to Saunderton station with the 3.43pm stopping service from High Wycombe to Aylesbury.** *J. D. Edwards*

Below: **A winter view of Saunderton Bank taken in 1961 as an unidentified 'King' climbs the 1 in 164 gradient up to the summit with a 13-coach service to Wolverhampton. With a 35mph speed restriction through High Wycombe followed by the long climb up the bank, speed was not the essence for down services over this part of the route.** *M. J. Esau*

Above right: **Another shot shows the 12.15pm service from Marylebone to Manchester as it climbs up to Saunderton on 12 February 1957 hauled by Leicester (38C)-allocated V2 2-6-2 No 60878.** *J. D. Edwards*

Below right: **Newly allocated to ex-Great Central services, Class A3 4-6-2 No 60102** *Sir Frederick Banbury* **ascends Saunderton bank in July 1949 with the 6.15pm service, the 'Master Cutler', from Marylebone to Sheffield. Coaches eight and nine on this service were the not altogether popular Tavern Cars. Notice also its home depot Leicester painted on the bufferbeam of the locomotive.** *H. K. Harman*

Above: **'King' Class 4-6-0 No 6016 *King Edward V* (81A)** approaches Saunderton station with the 6.10pm service from Paddington to Birkenhead in July 1960. The large space between the down line and the fence is the trackbed of the old single line Wycombe Railway to Princes Risborough. *H. K. Harman*

Below: **An Annesley (16B)-allocated 9F 2-10-0 No 92132 on the 10.48am service from Eastbourne to Sheffield Victoria** approaches Saunderton Summit on 15 August 1964. The '9Fs' saw considerable use on passenger services at this time. *Gerald T. Robinson*

Above: **Once past Saunderton station the up and down lines diverge for a distance of about 2½ miles to Princes Risborough. The up line is seen here on 8 August 1960 as 'King' class 4-6-0 No 6027 *King Richard I* (84A) speeds through the cutting with the 9.31am service from Birkenhead to Paddington.** *M. Pope*

Below: **A Nottingham-Marylebone excursion hauled by 'B1' class 4-6-0 No 61186 from Leicester tops the bank at Saunderton in September 1948. The train is running on the down line due to engineering work.** *H. K. Harman*

Left: **Just prior to Princes Risborough the lines once again converge. The down line here runs on the formation of the original Wycombe Railway route. The up line was constructed in 1905. In the early 1950s an ex-LNER 'A5/1' No 69827 (Neasden [34E]) approaches Princes Risborough with a stopping service from Marylebone.** *Rev R. F. H. Hine*

Left: **Looking north from the same bridge on 30 September 1948 'King' class No 6008 *King James II* (84A), still sporting its number on the front buffer-beam, departs from Princes Risborough with a Birkenhead to Paddington service. No 6008 was one of the last 'Kings' to receive a smokebox numberplate.** *R. N. Johnston*

Below: **A pre-Nationalisation photo included for its rarity shows Gresley 'A4' Pacific No 28 *Walter K. Whigham* running through Princes Risborough with a down freight in October 1947. The locomotive, which was previously named *Sea Eagle*, had been renamed at Marylebone a day or so earlier and was working its way back to its home depot of Grantham.** *H. K. Harman*

Above right: **An ex-LNER 'K3' class 2-6-0 No 61913 from Gorton (39A) on a Woodford-Marylebone freight passes ex-GW '6100' class 2-6-2T No 6108 (81B) on shunting duties at Princes Risborough in April 1948. 'K3s' were regular performers on ex-GC freight services.** *H. K. Harman*

Below right: **An excellent view of 'L1' class 2-6-4T No 67715 (34E) standing at the down platform at Princes Risborough on a morning service from Marylebone to Haddenham in June 1948. The locomotive, although carrying its new identity, is still in LNER apple green livery. These early 'L1s' were apparently not as well liked by the ex-GC crews as the later versions.** *H. K. Harman*

Above: **Another apple green engine sporting its new BR identity, 'B1' 4-6-0 No 61192 from Leicester Central (38C), passes through Risborough in May 1948 with the down 'Master Cutler', the 6.15pm service from Marylebone to Sheffield.** *H. K. Harman*

Below: **A rather grubby and frosty 'Hall', No 5929 *Hanham Hall*, stands on the station avoiding line at Princes Risborough on 23 January 1963 with the 11.5am service from Langley Green to Paddington (Goods).** *Peter Stears*

Above right: **Looking south from the down island platform on 29 June 1957, modified 'Hall' class 6960 *Raveningham Hall* passes through with a down fast as a '4800' class waits with the local service to Aylesbury. Standing in the bay is railcar No W16 and 0-6-0PT No 5755 on services to Oxford and Watlington respectively.** *N. C. Simmons*

Centre right: **'King' class 4-6-0 No 6006 *King George I* (84A) speeds through Princes Risborough on 9 April 1958 with the 2.10pm service from Paddington to Birkenhead. Notice the upper quadrant signals here, a reminder that at this time the line was still jointly operated.** *R. C. Riley*

Below right: **In July 1957 a pair of redundant ex-LNER 'J15' 0-6-0s, Nos 65390 and 65405 from Cambridge (31A), were allocated to Aylesbury for branch line goods work. On 9 April 1958 No 65390 passes Princes Risborough North signalbox with the Watlington branch goods. Their sortie at Aylesbury was brief; No 65405 was withdrawn from service in June 1958 and No 65390 in December of the same year.** *R. C. Riley*

Above: **The down 'Master Cutler' service to Sheffield hauled by 'A3' No 60052 *Prince Palatine* (Leicester [38C]) departs from Princes Risborough on 18 June 1949. On the right is Risborough North box, now closed but preserved by the Chinnor & Princes Risborough Railway Association.** *H. K. Harman*

Below: **Class A5 4-6-2T No 69814 (34E) in early British Railways livery takes the empty stock for the 8.16am service to Marylebone through the scissors crossing at the north end of the station and into the up platform at Princes Risborough in October 1948.** *H. K. Harman*

Right: **BR Standard Class 9F No 92092 from Annesley (16B) makes its way through Princes Risborough on 26 September 1964 with an up class 8 freight from Woodford yard. The '9Fs' were regular performers over the joint line during the last 10 years of steam operation.** *Brian Stephenson*

Right: **Sporting a rather burnt smokebox door, Class B17/6 4-6-0 No 61651** *Derby County* **from Colwick (38A) departs from Princes Risborough in August 1948 with the Marylebone-Dorrington (Salop) milk empties.** *H. K. Harman*

Right: **The daily pick-up goods from Banbury to Acton hauled by '2251' class 0-6-0 No 2256 (84C) runs through the Vale of Aylesbury on its approach to Princes Risborough on 2 February 1952.** *J. F. Russell-Smith*

Top: **The down 'Master Cutler' service hauled by a Sheffield Darnall-allocated 'B1' 4-6-0 No 61311 passes under the Thame roadbridge at Kingsey near Haddenham in June 1948. Although the line here has been singled, this is still an excellent location for photography.** *H. K. Harman*

Above: **On the same day 'A3' Pacific No 60050 Persimmon speeds past as a light engine on its way back to London. Closer examination of the buffer-beam shows the engine is allocated to King's Cross.** *H. K. Harman*

Left: **'Castle' class 4-6-0 No 5075 Wellington on a Sunday morning service from Wolverhampton to Paddington passes the small Buckinghamshire village of Haddenham on 1 May 1949. On the right is Haddenham Church, the trees on the left being planted to screen the nearby Tythrop House from the railway.** *H. K. Harman*

4. The Branch Lines

The Wycombe Railway was incorporated by an Act of Parliament on 27 July 1846 to construct a 9¾ mile branch from High Wycombe to Maidenhead. Delayed because of financial problems, the single track broad-gauge line was opened on 1 August 1854 and from the beginning was leased to the Great Western at a fixed rent. There were five intermediate stations on the branch at Maidenhead Boyne Hill (closed 1 November 1871), Cookham, Marlow Road, Wooburn Green and Loudwater; Furze Platt Halt was not opened until 5 July 1937. During the period of this book passenger services were operated using ex-GW '6100' class 2-6-2Ts, with some '4800' class 0-4-2Ts operating the through services between Maidenhead and Marlow. Goods service were generally in the hands of either '5700' 0-6-0PTs or '6100s'. Steam-hauled passenger services over the line were withdrawn from 8 July 1962. On 5 May 1969 the remaining through services to Aylesbury were withdrawn and on 4 May 1970 the section between High Wycombe and Bourne End was closed to both passenger and freight traffic thus leaving Bourne End as a terminus station.

The Great Marlow Railway had opened its short branch from Marlow Road to Marlow on 28 June 1873. The two-mile-long branch contained no intermediate stations but the two similar names obviously caused confusion and on 1 January 1874 Marlow Road was renamed Bourne End. The Great Marlow Railway was taken over by the Great Western in 1897. The branch was operated using the auto-train principle and for many years the steam service to Marlow was hauled by ex-GW '4800' class 0-4-2Ts, and known locally as the 'Marlow Donkey'. The daily goods to Maidenhead was often hauled by either a '2251' class 0-6-0 or a

Below: **The old Wycombe Railway branch from High Wycombe to Maidenhead left the joint line just to the south of Wycombe station. The first station on the branch after leaving High Wycombe was at Loudwater, pictured here in the early 1960s as '6100' class 2-6-2T No 6122 (81F) arrives with a service from Oxford to Paddington via Princes Risborough and Maidenhead. Loudwater was closed with the closure of the section between High Wycombe and Bourne End on 4 May 1970.** *M. Yarwood*

'5700' class 0-6-0PT. Steam passenger services, which comprised an hourly interval service between Bourne End and Marlow, were withdrawn on 8 July 1962 and replaced by a single-car diesel-unit. Little change took place on the branch until 10 July 1967, when the old station at Marlow was closed and passengers services were switched to a new single platform station that had been erected in the old goods yard.

The Wycombe Railway extended its line from High Wycombe through to Princes Risborough and Thame on 1 August 1862, and to Kennington Junction on 24 October 1864. Built as a broad-gauge line, the whole of the section between Maidenhead and Kennington Junction was converted to standard gauge between 23 August and 1 September 1870. The station at Thame, which had a fine Brunel-designed overall roof, was the main intermediate station on the branch. Wheatley was also another important station, particularly during World War 2, when special ambulance trains worked by LNER 'B12' locomotives, with a GW pilot engine from Oxford, brought the injured to the station from where they were transferred to the nearby Military Hospital at Holton. Other stations were situated at Littlemore, Morris Cowley (opened 24 October 1928), Horspath Halt (opened 5 June 1933), Tiddington, Towersey Halt (opened 5 June 1933) and Bledlow. Passenger services over the branch comprised six each way daily and were generally in the hands of Oxford (81F)-based '6100' class 2-6-2Ts. The branch was also used by numerous freight and parcels services which, together with the occasional diversion, regularly brought ex-Great Western '2800' class 2-8-0s, 'Castles', 'Halls' and 'Granges' as well as the occasional Standard Class 9F 2-10-0 over the line. The branch was closed to passengers on 7 January 1963, but continued to be used for both freight and diversionary traffic until the section between Morris Cowley and Thame was closed on 1 May 1967. Currently, the section from Kennington Junction to Morris Cowley Freight Terminal is still open, but in recent years the Princes Risborough-Thame section has been closed.

The 7½ mile branch from Princes Risborough to Aylesbury which opened on 1 October 1863 was to all intents and purposes another extension of the existing Wycombe Railway line from Maidenhead. Built again as a broad-gauge line, the branch was converted to standard gauge between 13 and 23 October 1868. During the same year the branch was effectively extended through to Quainton Road and Verney Junction by the Aylesbury & Buckingham Railway. At Verney Junction the Aylesbury & Buckingham line connected with the London & North Western's Oxford-Bletchley branch. Up until 1891 the line was worked by the Great Western, but from 1 July of that year the Aylesbury & Buckingham was taken over and worked by the Metropolitan

Below: **A view from the down platform at Bourne End in 1959 shows 0-4-2T No 1448 (81B) standing in the bay platform with the connecting service to Marlow as 2-6-2T No 6115 (81B) waits at the down platform with a High Wycombe-Maidenhead service.** *Photomatic*

Above: **On Sunday 25 September 1960 0-4-2T No 1421 (81B) departs from Marlow with the 11.45am service to Bourne End. During the latter years of steam on the branch a number of different 0-4-2Ts were used on the service. No 1421 had previously been allocated to Plymouth Laira (83D).** *M. Yarwood*

Below: **Marlow was the sub shed of Slough (81B) which supplied the engines for the branch. The small shed is pictured here on 24 September 1960 as 0-4-2T No 1421 is prepared for its next working to Bourne End. The shed was closed to steam on 8 July 1962 when the autotrain was replaced by a single-car diesel-unit.** *M. Yarwood*

Above: **The small terminus station at Marlow on 24 September 1960; 0-4-2T No 1421 (81B) waits to depart with the through service to Bourne End and Maidenhead. This station was closed from 10 July 1967 when services were switched to a new platform which had been constructed in the old goods yard.** *M. Yarwood*

Railway. Until January 1895 services over the A&B line were hauled by a pair of LNWR locomotives that had been loaned to the Metropolitan. The section between Quainton Road and Verney Junction was not altogether successful and was closed to passengers on 6 July 1936.

The Princes Risborough-Aylesbury section at one time boasted three stations. Little Kimble was opened on 1 October 1863 and is still open, although now an unstaffed halt. Monks Risborough & Whiteleaf Halt was opened on 11 November 1929 and is also still open, but South Aylesbury Halt, which opened on 13 February 1933, was closed on 5 June 1967. At Whiteleaf the line runs close to the famous Whiteleaf Cross cut out in the chalk of the adjacent Chiltern Hills. Services were operated on the auto-train principle using ex-GW '4800' 0-4-2Ts and '5400/6400' 0-6-0PTs, some services running through from Banbury and High Wycombe. There were also through services to Marylebone, operated by ex-LNER 'N5' 0-6-2Ts, 'L1' 2-6-4Ts, ex-LMS Class 4 2-6-4Ts and Standard Class 4 2-6-4Ts. Services from Maidenhead via Bourne End also saw '6100' class 2-6-2Ts traverse the branch. The steam auto services, which provided an hourly interval service, were withdrawn from 16 June 1962 and replaced by DMUs, the service to Princes Risborough being extended to run through to Aylesbury.

The last of the branch lines emanating from

Princes Risborough was the Watlington & Princes Risborough Railway. This 8½-mile-long branch was opened on 15 August 1872, and ran along the northern edge of the Chilterns before terminating at Watlington. The original intention was to continue the line and link up with the Moulsford-Wallingford branch but the work was never undertaken. The line was taken over by the Great Western on 1 June 1883, but prior to this was operated as an independent company running into its own small wooden platform adjacent to the Great Western station at Princes Risborough.

The main intermediate stations on the branch were at Chinnor and Aston Rowant but rail level halts were opened at Bledlow Bridge, Lewknor Bridge and Kingston Crossing on 1 September 1906, and at Wainhill on 1 August 1925. Passengers services were withdrawn on 1 July 1957. During the 1950s the branch had four services daily in each direction operated using ex-Great Western '5700' class 0-6-0s from Slough (81B). Coal services for Chinnor Cement Works also brought ex-LMS Class 2 2-6-2Ts from

Aylesbury. The Watlington-Chinnor section was closed to goods on 2 January 1961 but the remainder of the branch as far as Chinnor remained open to serve the large cement works. This traffic ceased in 1990 and during 1994 this section was taken over and opened as a preserved railway by the Chinnor & Princes Risborough Railway Association.

Of the above ex-Great Western branches only the Princes Risborough-Aylesbury and the Maidenhead-Bourne End/Marlow sections are open, although the section of the old Wycombe Railway route from High Wycombe to Princes Risborough was incorporated into the new joint line during 1906 and is, of course, still open.

The final branch covered in this book runs from Chalfont & Latimer to Chesham. The line from Rickmansworth to Chesham was opened by the Metropolitan Railway on 8 July 1889. Interestingly, it was the Metropolitan's original intention to construct its station here some ½ mile out of the town, but to ensure that the station was constructed in the town centre rather than on the outskirts the businessmen of Chesham gave the Metropolitan the not insubstantial sum of £2,000.

For a short while Chesham became the terminus of the Metropolitan main line from London; it had been the Metropolitan's intention to continue the line and link up with the London & North Western at Tring but due to various problems this section was never built. The

Above: **In July 1973 the Great Western Society ran steam over the branch from Maidenhead to Bourne End and Marlow in celebration of the centenary of the opening of the Marlow Branch. Here on a rather wet 15 July preserved 'Modified Hall' No 6998** *Burton Agnes Hall* **from Didcot Railway Centre speeds through Cookham** *en route* **to Bourne End.** *A. Muckley*

Chalfont-Chesham line became a branch on 1 September 1892 when the Metropolitan opened its extension northwards from Chalfont Road through to Aylesbury. The four-mile-long single track branch, which is still open, winds its way along the picturesque Chess Valley via a series of reverse curves which, shortly after the line was opened, led some wag to remark that 'if you look out of the window you may see the tail light of your own train'.

The branch, which has no intermediate stations, was operated using steam traction right up until it was electrified by London Transport in 1960 as part of the Metropolitan Line modernisation scheme. As part of this scheme a new bay platform was constructed at Chesham. During the early 1950s passenger services comprised a half-hourly push-pull shuttle service in the hands of ex-LNER 'C13' class 4-4-2Ts, but these were withdrawn in January 1959 and replaced by ex-LMS Ivatt Class 2 2-6-2Ts. These lasted until electrification; the first electric passenger trains ran from 12 September 1960.

Left: **Furze Platt Halt was opened by the Great Western on 5 July 1937. It is seen here in 1959 as 0-4-2T No 1448 (81B) departs with a service from Marlow to Maidenhead.** *Photomatic*

Centre left: **Another shot of No 6998 *Burton Agnes Hall* as it passes Furze Platt Halt on 15 July 1973 with a return shuttle service from Bourne End.** *A. Muckley*

Below left: **Brighton Atlantic No 32425 *Trevose Head* (75A) approaches Maidenhead with the return 'Riverside Special' from Marlow to East Croydon on 29 July 1959. It is about to pass the site of the old station at Maidenhead Boyne Hill (closed 1 November 1871).** *M. Yarwood*

Above right: **At Maidenhead, the Wycombe Railway branch joined the main line just to the west of the station. In this picture '5600' class 0-6-2T No 6627 from Reading (81D) runs off the branch at Maidenhead on 3 April 1956 with the pick up goods service from High Wycombe to Maidenhead yard.** *M. Yarwood*

Below right: **A general view taken from the down main platform at Maidenhead shows 'Hall' class 4-6-0 No 4922 *Enville Hall* from St Philip's Marsh (82B) speeding through on 3 April 1956 with a service from Trowbridge to Paddington. The old Wycombe Railway branch can just be seen curving away behind the guard's van.** *M. Yarwood*

Left: A final view at Maidenhead on 3 April 1956 shows 'Castle' class 4-6-0 No 5083 *Bath Abbey* (82C) on the 7.5am service from Cheltenham to Paddington. Standing just behind the large station running in board is '6100' class 2-6-2T No 6129 (81D) on a service from High Wycombe.
M. Yarwood

Far left: The branch, which ran westwards along the northern edge of the Chilterns, had a number of rail level halts. One such halt was at Bledlow Bridge. It was opened by the Great Western on 1 September 1906 ostensibly for use by steam railmotors that had been introduced on the branch at that time. The halt is seen here on 21 June 1951 as '7400' class 0-6-0PT No 7442 (81B) arrives with the 5.48pm service to Watlington. *R. H. G. Simpson*

Left: A service to Watlington hauled by ex-GW '5700' class 0-6-0PT No 5755 (81C) stands at the bay platform at Princes Risborough on 27 June 1957. There were only four services a day in each direction by this date, passenger services being withdrawn from the branch from 1 July 1957. *N. C. Simmons*

Below left: One of the two main intermediate stations on the branch was at Chinnor. Looking down from the adjacent roadbridge '5700' class 0-6-0PT No 9781 (81B) departs from the cement works siding with some empty coal wagons. A limestone works was opened here by the Chinnor Cement & Lime Co in 1908. By 1919 the works were producing some 250 tons of cement a week. Lime production ceased in 1974 and the weekly coal train was withdrawn in 1990. Luckily this section of the branch survives and is now operated by the Chinnor & Princes Risborough Railway Association.
R. H. G. Simpson

Left: **The other main station was at Aston Rowant, pictured here on 8 September 1956 as ex-GW '5700' class 0-6-0PT No 3697 (81B) with autotrailer No W181 arrives with the 2.32pm service from Princes Risborough.** *Hugh Ballantyne*

Centre left: **Looking in the opposite direction ex-Great Western '4800' class 0-4-2T No 1473 from Banbury (84C) passes the site of Aston Rowant station with the LCGB 'Three Counties Railtour' on 3 April 1960. This section of the branch was closed completely on 2 January 1961.** *Courtney Haydon*

Below: **The rural nature of the branch can be seen in this picture as '5700' class 0-6-0PT No 9653 (81B) approaches Watlington on 30 September 1948 with the 1.55pm service from Princes Risborough.** *M. Yarwood*

Above right: **A view of the branch terminus at Watlington, taken on 21 June 1952. The branch service is in the hands of ex-Great Western '5700' class 0-6-0PT No 5715 (81B). Notice also the ex-GW travelling safe on the platform.** *R. C. Riley*

Below right: **Another view of the terminus taken on 3 April 1960 as No 1473 pauses in the platform prior to returning to Princes Risborough with the 'Three Counties Railtour'. On the right is part of the goods shed and on the left the carriage shed and the remains of the small coaling platform. Interestingly, many of the buildings seen in these two pictures are still** *in situ.*

Below: **During the big freeze in 1963 the branch required the assistance of the Wycombe snow plough seen here on 21 January 1963 as driver Johnny Bloxham poses for the photographer alongside '5700' 0-6-0PT No 3622 and '2251' class 0-6-0 No 2289.** *Peter Stears*

Bottom: **There were three intermediate stations on the branch: Monks Risborough & Whiteleaf Halt (opened 11 November 1929), Little Kimble (opened 24 October 1864) and South Aylesbury Halt (opened 13 February 1933). On 3 June 1962 0-4-2T No 1455 (84C) and autocoach *Thrush* stand at Little Kimble with the 10.35am service from Aylesbury. South Aylesbury Halt was closed to passengers on 5 June 1967.** *L. Sandler*

Above left: **The Wycombe Railway opened its 7¹/₂-mile branch from Princes Risborough to Aylesbury on 24 October 1864. On 27 May 1962 0-4-2T No 1455 (84C) runs off the branch and enters Princes Risborough with the 2.25pm service from Aylesbury.** *L. Sandler*

Centre left: **Against the backdrop of the Chiltern Hills 0-4-2T No 1455 (84C) approaches Princes Risborough on 10 June 1962 with the 2.22pm service from Aylesbury Town.** *L. Sandler*

Below left: **There were three intermediate stations on the branch: Monks Risborough & Whiteleaf Halt (opened 11 November 1929), Little Kimble (opened 24 October 1864) and South Aylesbury Halt (opened 13 February 1933). On 3 June 1962 0-4-2T No 1455 (84C) and autocoach *Thrush* stand at Little Kimble with the 10.35am service from Aylesbury. South Aylesbury Halt was closed to passengers on 5 June 1967.** *L. Sandler*

Above: **At Chalfont & Latimer a four-mile branch serves the Buckinghamshire town of Chesham. The single-track branch was opened by the Metropolitan Railway on 8 July 1889. During the 1950s the line was worked by Neasden-based Class C13 4-4-2Ts. Here on 3 April 1956 'C13' No 67416 (34E) approaches Chesham Bois with a Chesham–Chalfont service.** *M. Yarwood*

Left: **The same locomotive stands in the bay at Chalfont on 26 January 1958 with a Chesham service.** *K. Fairey*

Below left: **Driver Bill Reynolds of Neasden shed stands proudly alongside 'C13' No 67418 in the yard at Chalfont & Latimer in the early 1950s.** *Peter Stears*

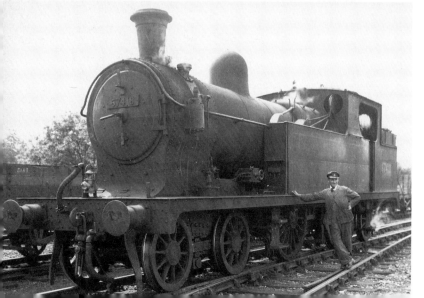

Above right: **Another 'C13', No 67420 (34E), stands at Chesham on 29 October 1950 with the branch service to Chalfont. As part of the electrification work a new bay platform was added at Chesham.** *Hugh Ballantyne*

Right: **A second view of the attractive terminus station at Chesham pictured here on Sunday 21 August 1960 as an ex-LMS Class 2 2-6-4T No 41284 (14D) departs with the 5.30pm service to Chalfont & Latimer.** *R. C. Riley*

Above: **The 'C13s' were replaced during the late 1950s by ex-LMS 2-6-2Ts. The line was electrified during 1962 and electrification work is still in progress as ex-LMS 2-6-2T No 41272 (Neasden [14D]) departs with the 3.2pm service to Chalfont & Latimer. No 41272 was the 7,000th locomotive to be built at Crewe.** *L. W. Rowe*

Below: **On 10 September 1960 No 41284 (14D) approaches Amersham Common with the 3.2pm Chesham-Chalfont service. The steam service was withdrawn and replaced by electric trains on 12 September 1962.** *M. Yarwood*

5. The Return to Steam

For a few years after the end of steam traction in 1968, BR established a steam ban over the whole system. Luckily common-sense prevailed and on 3 and 4 October 1971 the ban was broken by Messrs Bulmers who ran their 'Cider Train' from Kensington Olympia to Birmingham and back, hauled by preserved 'King' No 6000 *King George V*. The train returned to London via Bicester and High Wycombe. It was not until 1985 that steam was once again allowed back into London when on 12 January 1985 'A4' Pacific No 4498 *Sir Nigel Gresley* worked the 'Thames–Avon' express from Marylebone to Stratford. This signalled the start of a number of workings and between 1985 and 1990 a regular service of Sunday Luncheon trains was established. These ran between Marylebone and Stratford-upon-Avon via the joint line and were hauled by a variety of preserved locomotives from each of the big four companies, and once again the Chiltern Hills reverberated to the sights and sounds of steam.

On the preservation front during 1994, the Chinnor & Princes Risborough Railway Association inaugurated passenger services once again over a section of the closed Watlington branch and for many years now the Quainton Railway Centre has established an extensive preservation site at Quainton Road station.

Below: **It does seem incredible that the following two pictures were taken 24 years ago. The first shot shows No 6000** *King George V* **approaching High Wycombe on 4 October 1971 with the return Bulmers Cider Special from Birmingham Moor Street to Kensington Olympia.** *Brian Stephenson*

Above left: **This second shot shows the same train speeding through Gerrards Cross also on the same day. The Pullman coaches had unfortunately been painted in a light green and cream livery.** *R. Hooper*

Centre left: **Ex-Southern Railway 'Merchant Navy' class 4-6-2 No 35028** *Clan Line* **stands at Marylebone at 6pm on Sunday 9 October 1988 with a six-coach test train to High Wycombe.** *G. J. Wiseman*

Below left: **Ex-SR 'West Country' class 4-6-2 No 34092** *City of Wells* **makes a fine sight as it crosses the ex-LMS main line at Swiss Cottage on 12 June 1988 with a special from Marylebone to Stratford-upon-Avon.** *D. Trevor Rowe*

Above right: **On 18 June 1988 the same engine climbs Saunderton bank, again with a Sunday luncheon special from Marylebone to Stratford-upon-Avon.** *D. Trevor Rowe*

Below right: **On 9 November 1991 'Castle' class 4-6-0 No 5029 Nunney Castle makes a fine sight as it passes Subway Junction** *en route* **from Paddington with the 09.55 special service to Stratford-upon-Avon.** *Brian Morrison*

Locomotive Allocations

Motive power for the lines covered in this book were obviously supplied by a number of depots. I have included allocations for just two: Neasden, because it supplied motive power for all of the suburban and some main line services from Marylebone, and Banbury, as in later years it provided motive power for both freight and passenger traffic over both the Great Central and the joint line. For those wishing further information on allocations at Old Oak Common, Slough and Southall, I have provided these in my book *Britiah Rail Super Centres London: the Great Western Lines* (published by Ian Allan).

Neasden
The Great Central sited its locomotive depot at Neasden. The depot which opened in 1899 contained six roads and a locomotive repair shop. Allocation in the early years included a large number of Robinson designs but by the 1950s many of these types had gone. Motive power reorganisation in 1958 saw the shed pass into Midland Region control, being recoded 14D. Gradually the ex-LNER types were replaced by ex-LMS and Standard locomotives, although four ex-LNER 'B1s' remained at Neasden until 3 March 1962. The depots close proximity to Wembley Stadium saw visiting locomotives from all regions use servicing facilities at the shed. Dieselisation of the local services saw the shed close on 18 June 1962.

Allocations (1949–1958 coded 34E;1958–1962 14D)   **Total 79**
(steam only)
2 October 1954

Ex–GW '4800' class 0-4-2T	1473
Ex–GW '5400' class 0-6-0PT	5409
Ex–LMS Class 4 2-6-4T	42222, 42225, 42328, 42374
Ex–LNER Class A3 4-6-2	60050 *Persimmon*, 60052 *Prince Palatine*, 60063 *Isinglass*, 60102 *Sir Frederick Banbury*, 60104 *Solario*, 60108 *Gay Crusader*, 60111 *Enterprise*
Ex–LNER Class B1 4-6-0	61001 *Eland*, 61077, 61083, 61116, 61136, 61164, 61206
Ex–LNER Class C13 4-4-2T	67416, 67418, 67420
Ex–LNER Class L1 2-6-4T	67740, 67747, 67748, 67749, 67751, 67752, 67753, 67758, 67760, 67761, 67762, 67767, 67768, 67769, 67770, 67771, 67772, 67773, 67774, 67776, 67778, 67779, 67780, 67781, 67782, 67783, 67784, 67786, 67787, 67788, 67789, 67792, 67794, 67795, 67796, 67798
Ex–LNER Class N5 0-6-2T	69257, 69259, 69273, 69302, 69315, 69318, 69341, 69350, 69354, 69359
BR Standard Class 4 2-6-0	76035, 76036, 76037, 76038, 76039, 76040, 76041, 76042, 76043, 76044

The two ex-Great Western locomotives, although officially allocated to Neasden, were outstationed at Aylesbury and serviced at Slough.

1 January 1962   **Total 62**

Ex-LMS Class 4 2-6-2T	42053, 42070, 42080, 42082, 42086, 42087, 42088, 42089, 42090, 42092, 42133, 42134, 42157, 42159, 42178, 42222, 42225, 42230, 42231, 42232, 42248, 42249, 42250, 42251, 42252, 42253, 42256, 42279, 42281, 42284, 42291, 42618, 42629
Ex-LNER Class B1 4-6-0	61077, 61136, 61187, 61206
BR 'Britannia' class 4-6-2	70014 *Iron Duke*, 70015 *Apollo*, 70045 *Lord Rowallan*, 70048 *The Territorial Army 1908–1958*, 70049 *Solway Firth*
BR Standard Class 5 4-6-0	73010, 73032, 73045, 73053, 73066, 73069, 73156, 73157, 73158, 73159
BR Standard Class 4 2-6-0	76035, 76036, 76037, 76038, 76039, 76040, 76041, 76042, 76043, 76044

Aylesbury Town **Total** 7

This was a sub-shed to both Neasden and Slough. The original single road broad-gauge shed was provided by the Wycombe Railway soon after the opening of the branch from Aylesbury on 1 October 1863. The shed was completely rebuilt as a two road open-ended shed by the GW&GC and M&GC joint committees in around 1906. It was closed to steam on 16 June 1962.

Records show that during the 1950s the following types were allocated to Aylesbury Town.
• one ex–GW '4800' 0-4-2T or 5400 0-6-0PT
• one ex–LMS Class 4 2-6-4T
• one 'L1' 2-6-4T
• two 'N5' 0-6-2Ts
• two BR Class 4 2-6-0s

During the 1950s a number of 'A3' Pacifics were still operating the top services out of Marylebone. The locomotives were allocated at both Neasden (34E) and Leicester Central (38C). Prior to the take-over of the line by the London Midland Region in 1958 the remaining members of the class still working on ex-Great Central services were all allocated away, the last, Nos 60049/102/104/106/107/111, leaving on 21 September 1957. For the record the list of 'A3s' allocated to ex-GC services is listed overleaf.

Ex-Great Western 'Hall' class 4-6-0 No 6904 *Charfield Hall* from Tyseley (84E) stands in the locomotive yard at Neasden on 19 March 1959. In view behind the 'Hall' are the old coaling plant and shed water tank; the new coaling plant can be seen on the right. *R. C. Riley*

No	Date and first shed	Date away
60039 *Sandwich*	10/56 38C	4/57 to 34A
60048 *Doncaster*	2/49 38C	11/53 to 36A
60049 *Galtee More*	2/49 38C	9/57 to 35B
60050 *Persimmon*	2/49 34E	7/55 to 34A
60051 *Blink Bonny*	2/49 34E	11/53 to 35B
60052 *Prince Palatine*	7/54 34E	8/55 to 56B
60054 *Prince of Wales*	2/49 38C	6/56 to 34A
60059 *Tracery*	3/51 38C	4/57 to 34A
60063 *Isinglass*	2/53 34E	6/56 to 34A
60102 *Sir Frederick Banbury*	5/49 38C	9/57 to 34A
60103 *Flying Scotsman*	6/50 38C	11/53 to 35B
60104 *Solario*	6/50 38C	9/57 to 34A
60106 *Flying Fox*	8/55 38C	9/57 to 35B
60107 *Royal Lancer*	6/50 38C	9/57 to 34A
60108 *Gay Crusader*	9/52 34E	7/55 to 34A
60111 *Enterprise*	3/55 38C	9/57 to 35B

The following allocations show how they were distributed:

January 1950   **Total 11**

38C   60048 *Doncaster*, 60049 *Galtee More*, 60052 *Prince Palatine*, 60054 *Prince of Wales*, 60102 *Sir Frederick Banbury*, 60103 *Flying Scotsman*, 60104 *Solario*, 60107 *Royal Lancer*

34E   60050 *Persimmon*, 60051 *Blink Bonny*, 60111 *Enterprise*

January 1954   **Total 12**

38C   60044 *Melton*, 60049 *Galtee More*, 60054 *Prince of Wales*, 60059 *Tracery*, 60107 *Royal Lancer*

34E   60050 *Persimmon*, 60052 *Prince Palatine*, 60063 *Isinglass*, 60102 *Sir Frederick Banbury*, 60104 *Solario*, 60108 *Gay Crusader*, 60111 *Enterprise*

January 1957   **Total 8**

38C   60039 *Sandwich*, 60049 *Galtee More*, 60059 *Tracery*, 60102 *Sir Frederick Banbury*, 60104 *Solario*, 60106 *Flying Fox*, 60107 *Royal Lancer*, 60111 *Enterprise*

Although not actually covered in the book, I have included allocations for both Woodford Halse and Leicester Central as locomotives from these two depots regularly worked over the southern section of the ex Great Central line.

Leicester Central
2 October 1954   **Total 24**

Ex–LNER Class A3 4-6-2	60044 *Melton*, 60049 *Galtee More*, 60054 *Prince of Wales*, 60059 *Tracery*, 60107 *Royal Lancer*
Ex-LNER Class V2 2-6-2	60820, 60863, 60878
Ex–LNER Class B1 2-6-0	61009 *Hartebeeste*, 61028 *Umseke*, 61088, 61092, 61141, 61163, 61185, 61187, 61298, 61299, 61369, 61380, 61381
Ex-LNER Class J11 0-6-0	64375, 64438
Ex–LNER Class J52 0-6-0ST	68839

16 May 1964 (as 15D)   **Total 6**

Ex–LMS Class 5 4-6-0	44847, 44848, 44984, 45335, 45342, 45416,

The shed was closed completely on 6 July 1964.

Woodford Halse (38E)

2 October 1954   **Total 43**

Ex–LNER Class V2 2-6-2	60817, 60831, 60871, 60879, 60890, 60915
Ex–LNER Class B1 4-6-0	61078, 61192, 61368
Ex–LNER Class J11 0-6-0	64324, 64327, 64330, 64331, 64364, 64388, 64388, 64418, 64428
Ex–LNER Class L3 2-6-4T	69050, 69069
Ex–WD class 2-8-0	90033, 90039, 90040, 90046, 90065, 90080, 90095, 90137, 90218, 90365, 90448, 90474, 90484, 90486, 90504, 90507, 90509, 90516, 90520, 90574, 90638, 90672, 90697

16 May 1964 (as 1G)   **Total 26**

Ex-LMS Class 4 2-6-4T	42082, 42250, 42251, 42252
Ex-LMS Class 8F 2-8-0	48002, 48005, 48010, 48011, 48027, 48061, 48081, 48088, 48121, 48336, 48385, 48387, 48517, 48517, 48527, 48654
BR Standard Class 5 4-6-0	73032, 73053, 73071, 73073, 73157, 73159

The shed was closed completely on 14 June 1965.

Banbury (84C)

The shed, which was constructed by the Great Western, contained four roads and was opened on 29 September 1908. The allocation mainly consisted of freight locomotives although various mixed traffic types formed part of the allocation over the years. In September 1963 the shed became part of the London Midland Region being recoded (2D) and gradually the ex-GW types were allocated away. During the last few years of its existence the shed provided some locomotives for Great Central workings. Banbury was closed to steam on 3 October 1966.

Allocations 84C (Steam Only)

2 October 1954   **Total 63**

Ex-GW '2251' class 0-6-0	2202, 2209, 2246, 2256, 2270, 2297
Ex-GW '2800' class 2-8-0	2805, 2812, 2816, 2817, 2827, 2834, 2835, 2847, 2850, 2857, 2886, 2897, 3819, 3831, 3859
Ex–Gw 'ROD' class 2-8-0	3020
Ex–GW '4300' class 2-6-0	5317, 5332, 5361, 5399, 7315
Ex–GW 'Hall' class 4-6-0	4977 *Watcombe Hall*, 4980 *Wrottesly Hall*, 4987 *Brockley Hall*, 5930 *Hannington Hall*, 5947 *Saint Benet's Hall*, 5950 *Wardley Hall*, 5954 *Faendre Hall*, 5967 *Bickmarsh Hall*, 6906 *Chicheley Hall*, 6929 *Whorlton Hall*, 6966 *Witchingham Hall*, 6976 *Graythwaite Hall*, 6979 *Helperly Hall*
Ex-GW '5100' class 2-6-2T	4102, 4149, 5170
Ex-GW '5400' class 0-6-0PT	5404, 5407, 5424
Ex-GW '5700' class 0-6-0PT	4631, 5724, 7763, 8787
Ex-GW 'Grange' class 4-6-0	6839 *Hewell Grange*
Ex-GW 'Manor' class 4-6-0	7823 *Hook Norton Manor*
Ex-GW '9400' class 0-6-0PT	8400, 8405, 8407, 8452, 8459, 9425, 9426, 9438, 9449
Ex-WD Austerity class 2-8-0	90313, 90579

1 January 1966   **Total 47**

Ex-GW '6600' class 0-6-2T	6697
Ex-GW 'Hall' class 4-6-0	6920 *Aldersley Hall*, 6951 *Impney Hall*, 6952 *Kimberley Hall*
Ex-LMS Class 5 4-6-0	44710, 44860, 44869, 44936, 44942, 45089, 45114, 45288, 45299, 45308, 45331, 45392, 45418, 45426, 45493
BR 'Britannia' class 4-6-2	70045 *Lord Rowallan*, 70046 *Anzac*, 70047, 70050 *Firth of Clyde*, 70051 *Firth of Forth*, 70052 *Firth of Tay*, 70053 *Moray Firth*, 70054 *Dornoch Firth*
BR Standard Class 5 4-6-0	73013, 73014, 73048
BR Standard Class 9F 2-10-0	92004, 92013, 92030, 92067, 92073, 92074, 92128, 92129, 92132, 92203, 92213, 92218, 92224, 92227, 92228, 92234, 92247

Shed Visits

Neasden — Sunday 5 January 1959

Ex-LMS Class 2 2-6-2T	41329
Ex-LMS Class 4 2-6-4T	42222, 42230, 42231, 42232, 42252, 42256, 42279, 42291, 42568, 42588, 42595, 42618,
Ex-LMS Class 5 4-6-0	44847, 44993, 45191,
Ex-LNER Class B1 4-6-0	61028 *Umseke*, 61077
Ex-LNER Class L1 2-6-4T	67752
Ex-LNER Class N5 0-6-2T	69257, 69319, 69341
BR Standard Class 5 4-6-0	73157, 73159
BR Standard Class 4 2-6-0	76035, 76037, 76038, 76039, 76041, 76042, 76043
BR Standard Class 4 2-6-4T	80059, 80083, 80138, 80140, 80142, 80143

Leicester Central — Sunday 24 January 1960 Total 12

Ex-LMS Class 2 2-6-4T	40165, 40167
Ex-LMS Class 5 2-6-0 ('Crab')	42897
Ex-LMS Class 5 4-6-0	45006
Ex-LMS Class 3 0-6-0 ('Jinty')	47442
Ex-LNER Class V2 2-6-2	60815, 60863
Ex-LNER Class B1 4-6-0	61142, 61381
BR Standard Class 5 4-6-0	73045, 73053, 73066

Woodford Halse — Sunday 6 December 1959 Total 41

Ex-LMS Class 4 2-6-2T	42335, 42349
Ex-LMS Class 4 2-6-0	43063
Ex-LMS Class 3F 0-6-0	43330
Ex-LMS Class 8F 2-8-0	48220, 48318
Ex-LNER Class V2 2-6-2	60954
Ex-LNER Class B1 2-6-0	61028 *Umseke*, 61078, 61085, 61094, 61186, 61187, 61192, 61281, 61368
Ex-LNER Class B16 4-6-0	61473
Ex-LNER Class K3 2-6-0	61804, 61809, 61824, 61832, 61838, 61842, 61843, 61882, 61891, 61966
Ex-LNER Class J10 0-6-0	65158
Ex-LNER Class L1 2-6-4T	67771
Ex-WD 'Austerity' class 2-8-0	90033, 90065, 90125, 90218, 90299, 90433, 90504, 90524, 90638
BR Standard Class 9F 2-10-0	92010, 92069

Banbury — Sunday 24 January 1960 Total 40

Ex-GW '2251' class 0-6-0	2248, 2297
Ex-GW '2800' class 2-8-0	2858, 3816
Ex-GW 'Hall' class 4-6-0	4942 *Maindy Hall*, 5921 *Bingley Hall*, 5966 *Ashford Hall*, 5989 *Cransley Hall*, 5997 *Sparkford Hall*, 6906 *Chicheley Hall*, 6907 *Davenham Hall*, 6911 *Holker Hall*, 6915 *Mursley Hall*, 6924 *Grantley Hall*, 7905 *Fowey Hall*
Ex-GW '4300' class 2-6-0	5375, 6307, 6311, 6387, 7305, 7315
Ex-GW '5100' class 2-6-2T	4149
Ex-GW '5400' class 0-6-0PT	5407
Ex-GW '6400' class 0-6-0PT	6403
Ex-GW 'Grange' class 4-6-0	6840 *Hazeley Grange*
Ex-GW '7200' class 2-8-2T	7247
Ex-GW '9400' class 0-6-0PT	8452, 8498, 9449
Ex-LMS Class 8F 2-8-0	48430
BR Standard Class 5 4-6-0	73051
BR Standard Class 4 4-6-0	75000
Ex-WD Austerity class 2-8-0	90069, 90218, 90317, 90630
BR Standard Class 9F 2-10-0	92212, 92214, 92226, 92227